AF442033

# Contractors CANNOT Build Your House

*How to Save Money and Stay on Schedule When Building Your Home,*

*By Understanding the Process of Hiring an Architect*

Bryan Toepfer, AIA, NCARB, CAPM

ISBN: 9798639105715

Cover design by: Bryan Toepfer, AIA, NCARB, CAPM

Library of Congress Control Number: 2018675309

Printed in the United States of America

*To my wife Nicole, who has supported me in every risky decision I've made and who supported me the whole time in this endeavor, and every other difficult part of my career. Thank you for reading this book multiple times and helping me at every step.*

# Table of Contents

# Table of Contents

# Table of Contents

# Table of Contents

# Introduction:

So, You're Going to Build Something…How the Hell Do You Start?

You decided to finally begin that big project. Congratulations! Maybe it's time to start building your dream home that you've been thinking about for years, or putting an addition onto your existing home, or perhaps something as small as demolishing that horrible bathroom you can't tolerate and finally redesigning it. No matter the size or apparent "simplicity" of your project, chances are that you are beginning to become intimidated by what you need to do to get it done.

If you are reading this book, you most likely came to the realization that most of the country already did, or someday will…you have no idea what is involved in Design and Construction. This is not at all a poor reflection on you or anybody else. The Architectural and Engineering world have done a poor job of sharing with everybody what it is we do and what value we add. Over the years Architects and Engineers have become more and more isolated in only working with those already in our realm of Design and Construction, which only further adds to the problem that a large percentage of Construction and clients are left in the dark about their homes.

This in turn leads to most clients reaching out to a Contractor or Builder for all their questions, concerns and pricing. Contractors are vital to your project, and I have worked with some amazing ones over the years.

However, only engaging a single Contractor for your project would be equivalent to going to court without a lawyer. It certainly can be done, but you don't need me to tell you that's not in your best interest. It also has a severely low chance of success.

Having said that, I would like to get a disclaimer out of the way. If you are a Contractor and you made it past the title without ripping this book up, thank you first and foremost. This is not a manifesto of hate speech against Contractors. As I said a few sentences back, they are vital to any project. The point I want to get across more than anything else however, is they CANNOT be the only part of your project. In fact, further on we will demonstrate that they are very rarely are the sole contributor of a project. Many times, Architects and Consultants are still involved in a project, but hired by the Contractor instead of you, the client.  (Which ends up costing SIGNIFICANTLY more money.)

Moving forward, the format of the book will be under the assumption that your project is the Design and Construction of a brand-new home, as it is the most encompassing Residential project you could take apart in. Everything discussed however is just as relevant for any project you may be contemplating. I have broken this book into seven sections, based around the five phases of a project, as well as a very common phase prior to and after the project itself.

If I was successful in one thing with this book it would be this…**You won't be able to take on the role of an Architect, Engineer or Contractor just by reading this book. (If I did a somewhat decent job explaining everything, then you won't want to either.) But you will be much more confident on what the process looks like, as well as what to expect and how you can keep your project on budget and on schedule.**

While reading you will come across terminology unique to the Construction world. Second only to the Medical field, Construction has its own language and terminology. Many who have been engrained in this realm long enough can't help but to talk in a way that is off putting to many of those who don't live in the world of Construction every day. This book avoids an excessive use of these terms to keep it accessible, however when the need does arise to use one of these terms, I will provide an explanation following, no need for a dictionary.

On the following pages I will offer an explanation on why I did this and where this book came from. Following that, is a quick primer on what an Architect is and what they do. You can admit that you only have a vague idea on what we do every day, I have heard it from many clients I speak with, often less politely.

Good luck. As I say to all my clients when they are about to enter Construction; If you keep an open mind, and you stick with this to the end, you will understand more than you ever have when its complete.

# <u>Who Am I and Why Did I Do this?</u>

I do feel it helpful to come right out with why I felt this book needed to exist. As an Architect who opened his own firm, I saw an opportunity to serve an underserved market that has often been ignored from most established firms. I can recall quite often sitting at my desk at MULTIPLE firms, listening to phone calls come in from those looking for some guidance on their Residential projects, only to be stopped mid-sentence and told they should contact another firm. When I went off on my own however, and began trying to serve those building a new home or addition, etc., I found that a large majority had already been talking with a Contractor or Builder and were greatly misled or even lied to, as well as a very large number of those willing to admit they have never been involved in a Construction project and had no idea what to do next or even where to start.

After doing some research on existing books, literature and other sources, it became clear there is very few credible sources available to even explain what clients are about to get themselves into. This only left most people with two options: speaking with local Contractors, or internet searches which led to pages sponsored by certain products or Home Remodeling shows. I will reserve my rants about television programs related to Construction to a minimum, however over the years these shows have done irreparable damage.

Despite this uncertainty of walking away from a stable and comfortable job, I had the same reasons for doing so that also required me to take a shot at creating this guide. Mainly, the failings of the Architecture industry in general in the task of getting out there and educating the world on not only WHAT WE DO, but also educating the public in what they NEED to do when they take on this endeavor.

Many consider a Construction Project but get nervous when they hear some intimidating stories. You've no doubt come across a story that made you nervous to start Construction:

- An elderly woman is swindled out of her entire savings for a Construction Project that never happens and has no recourse because it's never been easier for someone to create a new corporation and disappear from their old one.
- Someone has hired an Architect who then rode off into the sunset and came back months later with some drawings and hand stretched out for money to be paid, all the while the client learned NOTHING and contributed just as much.

Countless other horror stories exist, and they all share one thing in common. The world of Residential Construction and Design has been largely ignored and has fallen into a state of "lawlessness."

Once I started my own firm, I hit the ground running to get out there and educate whoever I could. All of my efforts (listed in the "About the Author" section) were immensely satisfying to take part in, but it dawned on me that all these activities involved those already in the field of Design or Construction, and didn't branch much out in the world of clients…the audience that needed it the most. I began blogging on my website about the world of Architecture with the maturely named "What the Hell is Architecture?" series. As fun as this was (and still is) I began to wonder if any value was gained in this. Creating content on the internet to reach an audience is like throwing a paper airplane across the ocean to Asia, there is a potential group of billions who can receive your message, but there's a pretty significant chance they'll never see it.

One day I received a call from a client who was looking for some literature on converting their existing Garage into a usable living space, and they came across one of my posts discussing this process. They not only read it but found value in some of the other pieces I uploaded. It may have been "reaching" on my part, but I saw this as the confirmation that there are many who do not know what is involved in Design and Construction, and even less resources out there to explain it to them.

This is when I sat down and began writing this guide. I would sit down and think of all the questions I had to answer for clients that day and begin explaining those answers in fuller detail in these pages, all while my dogs and cats fought for my attention the whole time. At the end of the night, my wife would be gracious enough to read what I wrote and then patiently explain to me for the hundredth time all the apostrophes I missed and how horrible my run-on sentences were. But after all that, here we are. I truly hope you find some guidance in these pages; nobody should navigate such an intimidating process blind. Thank you for taking the time to read through this, and I can't wait to see how your dream home looks when its finished.

# What Is an Architect, and What Do They Do?

I already know you asked this question before even reading this book. In fact, the thing most clients are saying that really lead to this book's creation is the following… **"We are trying to save money, so we figured we can just have the project built without drawings."**

First, nine out of ten people assume that being an Architect is solely drafting Floor Plans, when this is only a very small facet of our involvement in projects and Construction. Second, any project that is built without drawings is most likely violating at least a few laws. Most Construction requires official documents submitted for building permits or approval from your local building department. If you are sold on the idea of building without getting caught, (which is terrifyingly how many proceed sometimes) then you are exposing yourself to risks and legal action down the road when you are inevitably caught, which you will be. There are government employees dedicated to finding these projects.

Finally, hiring an Architect or Engineer is NOT an added cost, it is an INTEGRAL cost. What I mean by this is many people mistakenly think the fee of an Architect is an added burden on their budget, however the opposite is true. Not only will the price of Construction be significantly lower when an Architect is involved but will often be lowered significantly enough that you will SAVE more money.

**Simply put, hiring an Architect does not cost more, it will actually save you money.**

But there is plenty of time in this book to explain how an Architect is going to be guiding you through the gauntlet of Design and Construction. One thing worth discussing here is what it takes to become an Architect as it is a professional licensed field. In order for an Architect to earn their Architectural License; they must not only earn a college degree, they intern for a few years under the supervision of an Architect and must prove they have gained experience in every facet of Architecture, they then finally have to take six of the most grueling exams known to man. (Sorry, but I had some nasty flashbacks to when I was earning my own license.) The fun doesn't end there though, every year Architects must meet a minimum number of continuing education hours or else lose their license to practice.

This last criterion is something that becomes invaluable to you as a client. The world of Construction is always changing and never sits still. Sure, there are often trends and fads that dominate for a decade or so, but everything else is truly dynamic and changing on a constant basis, a few things that always must be fresh in an Architect's mind are:

- Every day there are new products and materials being developed.
- New Codes and Guidelines are published regularly.
- Updated Construction methods evolve constantly.
- Legal precedents are changed with every Construction project.

An Architect's value however is not just derived from the difficulty they had in obtaining their license, or the need to stay up to date on best practices. An Architect's value is the fact that they are YOUR Representative during the entire phase of Design and all the way through Construction. There are not only ethical obligations to always act in your best interest, there are enforceable standards and even a policing body of Architects watching and enforcing these standards. Construction is expensive, stressful and difficult to keep an eye on; you need someone in your corner, or you are destined to become a tragic story of loss and financial ruin you read about too often online.

For those who do reach out to me, their first question is always the same, what will this cost? The short answer is 10% of your budget. It's never this simple though, there are many caveats to this. First of all, its 10%

of a REALISTIC budget, I know it's not fair to assume everyone has accurate cost data for their theoretical project, but if you have $200,000 set aside for a home that is going to cost $500,000 then $20,000 isn't going to cut it sadly. You, along with everyone else, most likely did an internet search before asking this though and were given a range of 5% - 15%. What never gets considered is where this data is coming from. I won't name any names, but the sources I found these numbers at were all skewed towards the creator being a Contractor or Builder. It's nice that they are trying to help but giving you incorrect information isn't doing you any favors. The lower end of that range only applies to LARGE projects, where conversely the larger percentage is for small projects. It's tough to explain sometimes, but the same amount of work and effort can be required for a tiny project as a project that is much larger, so your smaller project can seem to cost "more."

There is a lot of discussion needed to get to the "price" of your project. But after fielding hundreds of calls on this topic, I have a cheat sheet:

- The cost of bringing an Architect and their Sub-Consultants on board is 10% of your budget.
- Invoices are sent out weekly or biweekly and must be paid.
- ALL invoices must be settled before documents are sent.

- NO, you cannot have the price lowered to match another firm. Hire the other firm if price is all you're considering.
- You are welcome to have a Contractor hired, if you finish this book though you hopefully will realize this as a mistake.

If any of the bullet points above didn't sit right with you, give me to the end of this book and then we can revisit those thoughts. I won't use too many quotes from others in this book, but there is one quote from Red Adair I must ask you to consider with an open mind…

**"If you think it's expensive to hire a professional to do the job, wait until you hire an amateur.**

# <u>Part One:</u>

Programming and Analysis

*5% – 15% of Architectural Fee*

The first course of action you need to take is a portion of the process that is usually not considered part of the "Basic Services." (A term used to describe the phases of a project an Architect is involved in.) Programming and Analysis, the title itself tends to be confusing for some. Programming often brings to mind the idea of writing computer code, but the premise is not all too different for your project. Programming is defined as researching and identifying the problem your project is trying to solve. A more concrete definition is the process of determining what it is you are trying to build, specifically what rooms are needed, sizes, special requirements, etc. What are the things needed to make this your dream home?

Analysis is simply what it sounds like, analyzing and learning what you can about the project, often with a focus on the site itself. This phase leads to more confusion than any other process, which is not a great start for most clients as it's before the project even begins. This frustration and confusion always derive from the same thing, the fact that there is some work and investment required from the clients before engaging an Architect or Contractor.

It does need to be brought up at this point that the site for your home is not just some land you place the building on, it is an integral part of the project. I have fielded many phone calls and meetings with people who are either looking for plans for a home to be placed at some property in the future, or somebody who has drawings of a house they like or had and want to place it on a property in the future. It's never great to hear, but it doesn't work that way. I will avoid writing in an overarching pretentious Architectural view on the harmony between a building and its surrounding site, (although it is worth stating that the two should enrich each other) but from a purely technical viewpoint, the site your building sits on effects some very costly aspects of your home: The foundation system of your home, the orientation of it on the site, the HVAC system, (responsible for heating and cooling) stormwater management, and countless other aspects all depend on the site itself.

But whether I've convinced you on the value of your home design with site itself or not, the question is how does this impact you? What it means is that you will need to have a site purchased or at the very least a site you are considering for your project. I will discuss a question that you may have just asked, can the house be designed, and the site chosen later? Yes, however you cannot just take a set of drawings and have that project placed down on any site. Even with a completed set of drawings, there still needs to be some detailing on applying that building design to a site you finally purchase. You probably asked why that is, so I will give a drastic example. When placing the foundation to a house, it must extend far enough below the soil to be below the "Frost Depth." (The distance below the ground where the groundwater is not affected by the temperature of the air above the soil.) In parts of Texas, this depth only needs to be around one foot. If that same foundation system was built somewhere in Upstate New York, where the Frost Depth could be as deep as three or four feet, then after a single freezing night the ground would freeze and swell, and the foundation system would begin failing…which leads to some very scary structural problems.

Now locking down a site or even purchasing it before you even begin the project is not a great position for clients to be in. I hear it many times a week, where people want to make sure their project is feasible before they purchase their site, or even start hiring some professionals needed at this phase. (We will discuss shortly.) This phase is where you research this exact dilemma of whether you have a realistic goal in mind. The main questions that you are looking to have answered are as follows:

1.  What are the rooms, sizes and other design requirements?
2.  What is the general size of your home and where is it on the site?
3.  How will local Building and Zoning Codes affect your project?
4.  Do you have the money to even consider this project?

We will address each of these four questions in more detail in the following pages. I want to take this time to address a question that you have already asked in your mind, and one I have to discuss a few times a week…Having all this research and preparation done will cost money, and it does need to be done before you begin. I will avoid using these pages as a soapbox to keep hounding you to hire an Architect, but for your sanity and for your project's success and finances you need to hire a professional that lives, breathes and sleeps the above-mentioned items.

# What Are the Rooms, Sizes and Other Design Requirements?

This question tends to have already been answered by most clients I speak to. You most likely haven't thought of a specific breakdown of what rooms you want and how big they are, but I would wager you have an overall square footage size of the house you want. Very similar to everyone comparing how much weight they can bench press to determine strength, despite it only being one number among hundreds of different ways to compare strength, square footage of a house has become a standard metric that everyone uses to discuss homes. The overall square footage is a great start, but it is only a start in understanding your home.

Having a square footage in mind is in no way a bad thing. It offers a start for a conversation between an Architect and client. However, it's answering the question that hasn't even been asked yet; what is needed to make your house successful for you? The first step would be having the conversations that begin to distill what it is that your dream house is comprised of. When you daydream about this house, chances are you don't fantasize about the size of it. More realistically, you probably envision what it is like entering the house, and how you experience different spaces or even what you and your family might be doing in this dream home on a daily basis…All of these things that are not derived by the square footage, but in fact will dictate what that final square footage needs to be.

Now the task of compiling a Building Program and list of rooms does not seem very daunting. It's perfectly natural that you probably just asked out loud "Why the hell would I pay an Architect to do that, I can just set up an Excel spreadsheet." The challenge here however is not the task of creating a list of rooms, the challenge here is to graphically document the things that make your dream home a dream. Many clients when this Programming discussion starts, tend to fall back on the default setting of what rooms the house should have, and 99% of the time it's a rehashing of the house they live in. This isn't a lack of imagination on their part, it's simply an inherent tendency in humans to create from a bank of things they have experience with.

To put that simply, if I asked you to design a shoe in your mind and explain it verbally, you'll create a copy of the shoes your wearing. Because you've seen them a lot and associate them with shoes. The same is true for a house, you live there every day and when given the chance to create a new one, it will be assembled with all your associated elements you see every day. I am guessing that you are not willing to sink all this time and money into your new home for it to just be a shinier version of the house you clearly are not as thrilled with, this is where the Programming discussion can truly start crafting your fantasy home.

As I mentioned before, the square footage of your house should not be the starting point of this analysis, it should be the destination. This is also a cultural mindset in our country that is very tough to "battle." The size of a home seems to be inherently tied to its quality. Whenever somebody is bragging on television about their luxury home, or someone is bragging to their friends on the square footage of their new house, higher square footage is instantly the first metric of success we judge these houses on. Sadly, this is far from the truth. Between Architectural work and performing home inspections, I've seen gorgeous homes that would bring envy to anyone that are only 1200 square foot. I've also toured mansions over 5000 square foot that would impress nobody. If a larger house is what you want, or it's what is deemed necessary for success during Programming, then there is absolutely nothing wrong with that. The size needs to be arrived at from research and analysis, not forced for social status or as an attempt to "keep up with the Joneses."

Now despite all my language about not obsessing about the size of your house, a large majority of this section has been about determining sizes when Programming. The aspects of your dream home are often not related to size, however. It is certainly important to end up with an outline of what rooms are needed and how big they will be, but there is so much more that you desire in your house, even if you didn't realize it:

- Are there certain views you want to capitalize on?
- Are there portions of your house that you want to be able to expose to the natural elements in certain seasons?
- Do you want an indoor pool with a swim up bar and an attached movie theatre? (Be ready to pay if this last one is something you want, although if you're like me it's something you would love)

It's understandable that you may not have every single aspect of your house to be designed in your head at this point, in fact it's downright unrealistic at this phase. At the end of this part, what you should have is a Building Program, a graphic or outline stating what elements of your house need to be designed, and eventually built. What you will NOT have is the actual design of your building, that comes in the next phase; Schematic Design.

# What is the General Size of Your Home and Where is it on the Site?

After the somewhat convoluted process of trying to take your hopes for the new home and get it into a document listing all its rooms and components, you will have the "approximate" size of your dream home. Approximate is deliberately in quotes in the previous sentence, as right now is the most optimistic time for your project, and chances are you are going to need to make some compromises and perhaps thin out your "dream" list. In all my meetings with clients, I've never seen someone who started too small and needed to add to their Building Program, unfortunately it is ALWAYS the opposite.

Your next course of action would a quick graphic analysis of the building size, number of floors in your home and an understanding of where it will sit on your site. It's at this point where I will reiterate that this is NOT the part of designing your building. Through no fault of their own, many clients have become concerned over seeing a large box on a site plan representing their dream home. This is simply showing the size of the building and where it would sit, I won't speak for all Architects, but a large majority don't tend to design square homes. Although the cost savings in Construction would be astronomical if we did, but I'll wager your dream home doesn't tend to be a large square.

At this point we've mentioned a few times the terms Site Plan, and what that is an overall plan of the site itself. This often is the most jarring part of the initial conversations I have with clients, (excluding money, which I will get to soon) as the fact is many people don't realize they need to be providing a site and the appropriate documents, most importantly, the Site Survey. The Site Survey is a drawing that provides the boundaries of the property, measurements and locations of existing structures, underground utilities perhaps and the Topography (contours and shape of the land) of the site itself.

This document is not readily available, while most municipalities have property plans regarding the boundaries for tax reasons, all the other information needs to be gathered from a LICENSED Surveyor. I did not capitalize licensed simply for effect, this Site Survey provides a lot of important information for design professionals. Therefore, it must be prepared by a Surveyor who has undergone training, experience, and examination. The same goes for Architects and Engineers, sadly I have a lot of clients who saved money by working with an unlicensed individual in any of these fields. But when it comes down to it, an unlicensed individual has no ethical or professional liability or any obligations to your project. Without earning their license, they have most likely not reached the level of knowledge and experience needed for your project's success either.

The jarring moment with clients at this part is not that they need to get the Site Survey, it's the fact it does require hiring a licensed professional to visit the site for a few days and take a few more days creating the drawing. It requires a financial commitment at this point and that does tend to be daunting for some. I am not a surveyor, so any cost data I provide I ask you to follow up with an actual Surveyor. However at the time of writing this, I have seen many surveys cost around $1,000 an acre, so if you are planning on building on a large property, then hopefully reading this you can avoid the sticker shock I've all too often seen with clients.

But for some it isn't even the cost of this part that causes them to hesitate, it's simply the fact that they need to start committing to a site, eventually purchasing it. I hear it a few times a week, "We want to make sure the project is feasible before we purchase the property." Which is a valid concern, and we will certainly discuss using this phase as a chance to validate whether your budget will hold up with the realities of Construction. However, at some point if you continue forward, you need to make the commitment of a site. Getting all the way through the

Architectural design to have the perfect site be unable to be purchased at the last minute is a very disappointing conclusion for your dream home…not to mention the fact that all the professionals you hired throughout still get paid, whether your home is built or not.

If you've fantasized half as much about your dream home as most of the clients I speak with however, then purchasing the site and having a Surveyor document it is a small price to begin the process of turning that dream into a reality you come home to every night. At the conclusion of this part, you will have a Site Survey, as well as a Site Plan with an approximate size of your home and where it should sit on the site. The specific location and orientation of your building are both factored in during the next phase, Schematic Design. At this point, the approximate location is more attuned to how you want to experience the house and site. For example, if there is a large pond with a dense bank of trees that you want your house tucked into, this is the drawing to show that. As for the shape of the building and how it sits on the site to maximize sunlight, views of the water and proximity to trees, that comes in the next phase of Schematic Design.

# How Will Local Building and Zoning Codes Affect Your Project?

It's a tale as old as time, (try to avoid singing Beauty and the Beast) You purchase the property and start really seeing the opportunities it and your new home could provide…and then it turns out there is a local ordinance, or Zoning Code that does not allow what you want to do, even though it's completely harmless or trivial. Many clients have felt a surge of anger at this point when the Building, Zoning and Local codes begin to dictate and hinder what they want to do, and rightfully so. It costs money to buy the property, the taxes paid every year are usually significant, and now an outside force is making things difficult for them.

It is always worth hiring an Architect to perform a separate Code Analysis on a potential property before you even engage this entire phase of Programming and Analysis. The good news is any money spent on this report is money you will save if you were to continue with the full process. The bad news is after a few hours of analyzing and researching, an Architect can find that your project is either going to be too difficult or flat out impossible. Yes, I am aware that I phrased the bad news as good news as well, and that is intentional. Paying for a few hours of a professional's time for a project that cannot be built often seems like a waste, but how would you feel signing multiple contracts with different professionals and builders only to find out the project cannot continue?

Some of you may have already shouted the question, "Can't we file for an appeal?" I hear it every time the Local Ordinance begins causing some difficulties in our project's initial visions. The technical answer is yes, you can file for a "Variance," which is proving to the Authority Having Jurisdiction that you should be allowed an exception from certain ordinances. The answer I will give however is a resounding NO. You are certainly able to file for a variance, but in all my years of experience this is never an easy process, and it very rarely results in the exception being granted…and on the few occasions it is granted, I have never seen it applied to a Residential Project, more so for Commercial work or buildings deemed important for the community. Your dream house is certainly special to you, but sadly it means nothing to the public good or to the local Building Department.

If you truly are determined to stick with a site that has any restrictions on it though, and I understand that dream homes often have a dream site you would want to fight for, then you are going to need to hire an Architect in preparing some documents and drawings for your appeal. This may sound like preparing for a legal case, and while there will not be any cross examinations or surprise witnesses, it will be handled as such. I am always an advocate for hiring an Architect, but this can be somewhat of a commitment as the Building Department will usually not be able to make determinations from verbal explanations or hand gestures…they are going to need some more finished drawings and details. Even if the appeal is not granted and the site is abandoned, this work can of course be used elsewhere with some rework, just be mindful that some time and effort is required here.

At the conclusion of this part, you will have a Building and Zoning Code analysis that shows that your project is feasible, or at the very least any restrictions to be mindful of. Very rarely is there is no external elements that need to be considered in your design, every project I have ever worked on has had conditions to be met in the ways of Setbacks, (distance required from road to building) height restrictions, and often even material choices.

This is also a great time to begin conversations with the Local Building Department. Often, I speak with clients who want to keep their projects hidden, as if they were secrets needing to be protected. However, I will state my opinion on this clearly, the more communication you can have with your Building Department, the easier it will be in the future and the better conversations you will have. You will need to engage them no matter what when it comes time to submit your Stamped Permit Drawings, (drawings prepared by a Licensed Architect) better they know about the project throughout the process, opposed to having a set of documents thrown at them at the last minute. It's worth noting that Design and Construction are a series of "battles of give and take." Interacting with the Building Department is no different…discussing the possibility of using a material the town often forbids is much easier, and much more successful when you've been talking to each other for months and start to trust and know each other.

# Do You Have the Money to Even Consider This Project?

As much as I would naively love to believe you have been hanging on my every word, chances are you probably jumped straight to this question. I am not exaggerating when I say every phone call, or every meeting I have with someone for the first time, many aspects of money are what everyone wants to discuss: How much will Construction be? How much is it to hire an Architect? Are you willing to work for less than another Architect whose fee I was given? Hopefully you won't ask that last question. If you stick with me in the following pages, I can prove to you why this wouldn't be a great idea for the success of your project and Project Team either.

In the following chapters you will be seeing a recurring theme in the sense that throughout the Design and Construction of your project you will constantly be balancing the three factors of your project's success: Time, Quality, Budget. Everyone who's been working in the field for any amount of time has heard the joke that you can only pick two of them. However, I personally don't find that to be true IF you are realistic on all three accounts. Sadly, most people think only in terms of extremes. It becomes true when you have an unrealistic expectation of any of them. If you want your house to be built in a week or two, then the quality is going to be downright horrible and yet it will still cost a lot. If you are looking for the kind of insane luxurious upgrades that you will never notice again, then prepare for Construction to last much longer on the side of uncomfortable, and a bill that would bring tears to most. To bring this point much closer to home for most people planning their new home, if you don't want to spend money, then prepare for a shoddy building that will only disappoint.

Money may be the root of all evil, but at the beginning of your project it is going to be the overarching thought above all others. I can assume that you've noticed in just these first few pages, I've mentioned time and time again that most people starting this process will naturally reach out to a local contractor and ask them what it will cost to build a home. Because a price is usually provided, this seems like the easiest course of action. However, that price comes with a few caveats that you need to understand before finding yourself in a bad situation.

First of all, nobody can price a house without any drawings or design work done, if a price was provided to you without any of these items than you have just been charged a price per square footage that would knock your socks off if you knew it. The reason being that in order to anticipate all the unknowns and decisions the owner may make in the process; a large amount of money must be charged to cover any cost overruns on their end. After all, they are a business that must survive.

Second, anybody telling you they can build without drawings or plans is flat out lying to you. Ignoring the kind of talent it would take to plan and build a house out of thin air, there is the legal matter of submitting permit drawings to the Authority Having Jurisdiction for building permits and tax record keeping. You can't just build a house wherever; it needs to be documented with the government. Since a licensed Architect is needed for these stamped Permit Drawings, many builders or contractors use in house or favored Architects and Engineers for these drawings. While you may have just considered the ease of only hiring one firm to handle everything, you just paid a large premium as all the involved professionals' fees are determined without your involvement. This also ignores the fact the Architect is the Owner's Representative throughout the process and during Construction, but if their salary is paid by someone other than the Owner, then their allegiance has no choice but to be skewed. If that last sentence didn't hold much gravitas, then during the chapter of Construction we will continue to prove the severity of that situation.

But we will move past the discussion of why it is better to hire an Architect directly, I will drive that point home a few hundred more times in the following chapters. The Programming and Analysis phase is a great time to determine the difficult question of whether you have a realistic budget for your project. While it would be almost impossible to find a detailed budget with the limited design you have at this point, it is still possible to get some cost data to keep your numbers in check. During this phase you will have an overall square footage of your home, the Building Program, any code restrictions, and the site. With this information you will have enough to get some finely tuned cost estimates from a variety of sources.

The most basic one is simply applying a cost per square foot based on your location. This is a good way to quickly check if you are even in the ballpark with your budget. Speak to your Architect on what is a good square footage number, as they have a good database on what their projects have been costing to build. At the time of writing this in Upstate New York, $150 dollars a square foot seems to be a good mid-range number to use when planning. Having said that, that previous number has already become obsolete by the time I finish this page as Construction costs ebb and flow drastically. However, whatever range you come across; it's always tempting to plan with the low end in mind.

It's not rocket science; people always want things to be cheaper. But I am going to strongly advise you right now that you need to stick with the mid-range, or even higher end number as it is more realistic. Worst case scenario, things go unrealistically smooth and you end up with extra money, the opposite scenario is much more stressful.

Another avenue of getting cost information is to hire a Cost Estimator. That is a professional who does exactly what you would think, they are able to provide cost estimates at different phases of the project. Before you panic at the thought of the cost estimate changing at each phase, the idea is at the beginning of your project your price is the most "theoretical," as a lot of unknowns are still present. As you progress through the phases, more and more of the project will be completed and finalized, and thus the numbers become more concrete. If you hire the right Cost Estimator at the beginning, then your starting estimate will not only be within a better margin of "final" accuracy, but the number will only go down as the project becomes more fleshed out. I cannot stress enough the value that hiring a Cost Estimator will bring.

All too often I work with clients who have their starting budget and want to scrimp and save as much as possible and believe that wanting the project to fall within their budget to be enough. It pains me to type this, but when it comes time for Contractors to bid on your project, your hopeful budget means nothing. Unless the economy has taken any kind of downturn, Contractors are booked solid and usually over busy, so the price will be what they say it will be. Better to know you can afford it up front then after months of design and deliberation. With larger homes and projects, some clients make the mistake of thinking their project is large enough to warrant special attention. The harsh reality is it probably won't be. There is always more work and always larger clients for them.

I have said this so many times I often feel like literally shouting it from a mountaintop, but since I don't have the energy to climb a mountain, I'll have to use the space on this page…

## IF YOU TRY TO SAVE MONEY BY NOT HIRING <u>ANY</u> OF THE PROFESSIONALS NEEDED, YOU ARE ONLY GOING TO SPEND MORE MONEY AND HAVE MORE ISSUES.

The statement above applies to everyone; Estimators, Architects, even if you find the cheapest local handyman to save on Construction costs. I have so many horror stories of the damage these decisions have led to for others. Feel free to ring me up anytime and I'll gladly share them with you. This house is your dream…it's going to cost you hundreds of thousands of dollars and months of your sanity, you will live in it every day for the rest of your life if it's done right. This is not the item in your life you want to compromise on for a few pennies.

At the conclusion of this part you will have a Cost Estimate as well as your overall budget with a "Contingency Reserve." Contingency is something everyone forgets to account for, it is simply an amount of money that is not part of the budget, but is set aside for unknown factors, changes or even "missed" items. This needs to be at least 5% - 10% of your budget. Now I can already hear you yelling at this page, "I have to set aside $20,000 to cover mistakes made by the professionals I am paying all this money for?" (This scenario assumes your budget is $200,000.) This is never a great conversation to have with clients, especially because there is more involved than just covering omissions, every client I have had has wanted to add or change during the project, and I will wager that you are no different, so why not be covered for it?

This is also the wrong mindset to even consider. To ask an Architect for 100% drawings requires so much time and exploration of your project and property, it would not be worth your time. I know that probably didn't reassure you, so I will use a past project to demonstrate my train of thought here. When working on a $14 Million-dollar institutional project, there were months of preparing the drawings. When it came time for Construction, the amount of money required to simply prepare the site for all the utilities and buildings was over a Million dollars! During this preparation of the site, more than five feet under the ground in multiple locations were dumpsters filled with solid concrete. The removal of these insanely heavy dumpsters were not covered in anyone's drawings, and surely not in the Contractor's Bid. The cost to remove each of these dumpsters was a few thousand dollars each, but the cost and time to have a Civil Engineer or an Architect dig around the site in multiple locations to at least five feet below to have discovered these dumpsters would have been 100x more. That is a drastic example you most likely won't have in your home's Construction, but it highlights just how important a Contingency Reserve is. Plus, if you come out with some extra money when it's all said and done, I'm sure you won't mind.

# Conclusion of Programming and Analysis

You may have remembered a sentence I wrote in the first few pages how many people attempt to hire a Contractor without any of the documents and information created in the Programming and Analysis phase. Hopefully after reading the last group of pages, you can understand how difficult that makes the rest of the project. In fact, your project isn't going to move forward without the previous phase being completed, so I still scratch my head on why this has become accepted as a "preliminary" phase. If it feels as though it is too daunting to gather all the information previously discussed before speaking with your Architect, then most Architects would gladly include this in their services. I will save you the awkward conversation you may be wondering about having, yes all that takes some time and effort and therefore will need to be treated as an investment in your project.

It makes me cringe, but there are many people who try to move their project forward without Site drawings or an understanding of the Zoning Codes, some without knowing their budget. I could write multiple chapters on the spectacular ways those "projects" have failed, but I hope by reading this you have decided that you don't want your dream home to be an expensive regret down the road.

# Part Two:

Schematic Design

*10% – 20% of Architectural Fee*

The phase of Programming and Analysis never tends to be the most exciting for clients. There is certainly enthusiasm as a clear picture of what their project will become and how it will be successful starts materializing. However, besides a Site Plan with a square drawn to scale, the client unfortunately doesn't have many graphics or ideas of what their home will even remotely look like.

The next phase we will dive into is Schematic Design, and this is where the client's ideas begin to truly take form. This is also the phase that has the most communications back and forth between the Architect and the client. That tends to be very polarizing, many clients thrive on this level of involvement and changes in their future home, while just as many can easily become overwhelmed or even irritated when this begins to ramp up. I will strongly recommend having an in-depth conversation with your Architect on what your schedule is, how you prefer to communicate, (phone call, in person, e-mail, etc.) and agree on some recurring meeting schedule or design reviews at determined intervals.

Once the communications protocol is established however, this is undeniably the most "fun" phase for clients. That may cause you some concern as it's only the second of five phases, which would hint at the process becoming more stressful and only going downhill after here.

You wouldn't exactly be wrong, however that's why we're here right now, so you can be prepared and keep the whole process "fun"…except for Construction, which is very rarely that be enjoyable for clients, but we'll get through that when the time comes.

There are two types of clients who reach this point; those that have hundreds of images of houses, materials and styles they enjoy (whether gathered from Social Media, Internet, or in some rare occasions actual clippings from magazines) and those who have nothing to share and are honest about having no idea what they even want.

If you are truly coming to the table with a clean slate and looking to your Architect for their talent and expertise, there is no need for concern, many clients have started their projects this way and slowly evolved into naturally becoming involved. Rarely do clients grant us "carte blanche" (pretentious way to say complete freedom) with their dream homes, but there is a common misconception from many who are stressing about involving so much of their limited time and attention for the lengthy process of Design and Construction. Your involvement is up to you, there are certainly distinct points where you are required for the project to proceed smoothly, but at the same time you are paying a professional to provide a service. If you are looking for a consultant who can get your house ready to be built and you want to leave yourself out of the trenches, (and I am sure as you read this you may be getting that feeling) then that is a perfectly acceptable method.

If the idea of leaving your dream home in the hands of somebody other than yourself made you squeamish, then you can take comfort in knowing you are not alone. Often clients who are meeting with me for the first-time bring hundreds of images they have been curating for months, or even years. This can aid the design process, as there is often a pattern or theme in what images you saved that you may not even be aware of. Clients never realize it, but we all have our own inherent design philosophies, even those who are not "designers."

I am a firm believer that the more that people can react to, the better the final product will be and the smoother it will be getting there. Often, I have sent animations or renderings to clients at early stages that had more things they hated versus elements they loved. EVERY SINGLE TIME however this created a constructive conversation which not only put us on track and allowed us to progress even faster towards the end. There is occasionally confusion and sometimes anger as to whether or not I am finishing with a design they do not enjoy, always offer your criticism and elements you want changed, but do keep in mind this is an iterative process, it takes time and constant adjustments. I have had my share of projects that had very few initial communications and then the project was "off to the races" for final Construction Drawings, and they have been successful as well. A majority of those I speak with however want to stay involved and thoroughly enjoy bouncing ideas off each other throughout design, and your Architect should gladly function with this method choice.

Whichever way you want to proceed is your choice, just make sure you make your expectation clear when you meet your Architect. As you move through the phases (or if you glanced at the Table of Contents) you may have noticed that every phase is simply answering a series of questions about your home, and you would be correct! As I mentioned previously, this is the phase where you can finally start seeing how your home will look when built, and in doing so you can finally answer the questions below.

1.  What will the layout of your home be?
2.  What will your house look like on the exterior?
3.  How does your house interact with the site?
4.  Who will make up your project team?

# What Will the Layout of Your Home Be?

In the grand scheme of Design and Construction, there are hundreds of aspects of what is involved that most people are not even aware of. I brought this up earlier as a failure of our industry, and I do hold strong that it is getting worse every generation. However, there is one concept that is universally understood or at the very least part of the common knowledgebase, the Floor Plan. I have yet to speak with a client who has not either brought me some Floor Plans or were looking for one. I then often need to clarify that ALL projects do require more than just Floor Plans. In fact, I will use this moment to mention a nasty lie many clients I meet with have been fed by someone who they discussed building their project, the idea that all someone needs to get a project built is some Floor Plans. I'll explain the true error of this mentality with some facts, but this is so untrue and is setting you up for some nasty surprises and cost increases down the road. Back away from anyone who tells you this.

Our digital age has truly allowed for access to so many things we didn't have before, and Residential Design is no different. It has never been easier to find Floor Plans from other houses with just a quick search. Most clients I meet with bring at least one Floor Plan they like as a starting point for their project. I need to emphasize though that bringing Floor Plans is simply a STARTING point. I try not to project my personal opinions into meetings with clients, but it is worth stating that when spending the amount of money needed to build a new house, (the most expensive purchase anyone could make) it feels a bit regressive to build somebody's else's dream house instead of your own.

Now I can tell somebody reading the previous paragraph had to have scoffed, or at the very least rolled an eye or two. I don't mean to dismiss anyone of course, as I said there is nothing wrong with using other designs and drawings as a starting point for conversation. However, whether you agree with my opinion or not there is another reason you won't want to use another's design…you legally can't. Not only is it not common knowledge for those outside the industry, but it seems even some of those embedded in this Construction realm have been unaware of the legal issues of using others designs. **Architectural Design and Drawings are copyrighted intellectual property, and no require no filing or claiming by anyone to be treated as such.**

It's a tough conversation to have with clients, second only to disagreements about money, but when a building is built it is your property…but the design of it and the DRAWINGS themselves however are owned by the Architect. That last part tends to lend some confusion, as in almost every project the Architect issues drawings to the Owner and the Contractors. However, the drawings are only given permission to be used, they sadly don't belong to you. This only further supports my previous argument made in the previous chapter on why you can't use drawings for one project for a different site, there is not only detailing needed for each site, but those drawings cannot be used in any context or setting other than the Architect's initial design. After the shock of this wears off, the next question that is usually asked is "If we get permission from the Architect, can we use this design?" The answer to this is yes, if given permission from the Architect than a design can be duplicated or used elsewhere. A few things to consider:

- The Architect in question is losing business with this arrangement, so if they do allow this then there is going to be financial compensation required.
- The design or drawings you are "purchasing" rights for will still require some rework or designing for YOUR site, this will cost time and money.
- This arrangement MUST be captured in a contract, to avoid any claims or issues down the road.

If it seems as though I have a bias against this route it's because often this permission will not be granted by the Architect. Now that probably irritated you a bit, I know how angry it has made clients I have met with. It leads to a feeling that the Architect in question is being spiteful and only wants you to hire them instead. This isn't exactly wrong, as all the work that goes into a full set of Design and Construction Drawings is staggering, however financial motivations are not the primary concern in giving permission for others to use.

The biggest detractor for an Architect to allow others to use their Design or drawings is legal and professional liability. (Refer to the section on "What is an Architect, and What Do They Do?") But even the difficulty in earning our license is not what makes us hesitant to allowing other access to our drawings or designs, we are legally liable for a VERY long time (varies from state to state) on every drawing we stamp with our official seal. If a building fails, or a design doesn't meet federal accessibility guidelines, or any of countless other scenarios occur, we are called into court. If we are found to be negligent, then even our License, and therefore our livelihood is at risk.

While it can be tempting to scowl at "the greedy Architect" who won't let others use their work, the reality is the exposure is simply too great.

I have no problem allowing clients to use my designs elsewhere for a nominal fee IF I can maintain control of them when being adapted to another site or environment. Allowing someone else however to do so only increases my liability. They may be "taking it over," but if anything goes wrong then not only am I still liable, but they would tend to remove as much risk and blame as possible to save their own skin.

But putting legality, liability and everything else discussed aside, this is YOUR dream home and so chances are the Floor Plan you want can't exist yet, as you haven't had it created. There is more to your home than what the Floor Plan is, no project should (or probably can be) designed and reviewed solely in Plan drawings. With BIM (Building Information Modeling) and Virtual Reality technologies on the rise, it's never been easier to convey the "experience" of your home as well. During Programming you should have begun trying to put words and elements to how you want to experience your house, and here is the time to have it conveyed graphically. When clients look at Floor Plans, they tend to focus on the sizes of the rooms and locations of the windows, both very important aspects, however, here is the chance to start trying to imagine yourself walking through the house before it's even built. At the conclusion of this part, you should not only have a Floor Plan, but also a feel on the experience of the interior environment.

<u>What Will you Home Look Like on the Exterior?</u>

One of the very few things that home improvement shows on television have not completely distorted into outright lies to the general public is the importance of Curb Appeal, referring to the value of what your home looks like from the outside, or the curb of the street. However, before I give too much credit to these shows, how your home looks on the exterior is MUCH more than just trying to impress (or even one up) your neighbors. The exterior design of your home is just as integral to your dream experience as the interior layout and materials.

In my experience, many people have a much clearer idea of what they want the exterior of their house to look like versus the interior. You may not have a general idea of what rooms you want and how they interact with each other, but I would wager you have a pretty clear picture in your head on what your house looks like as you pull into your imaginary driveway and mentally see it. Just as I mentioned in the previous pages, it is perfectly fine to bombard your Architect with hundreds of images you have collected, and just as fine trusting your Architect with it all to save yourself the stress.

The site or neighborhood that your house is being built in however really becomes a critical factor at this point. During Programming and Analysis this context may have been reviewed simply from a standpoint of any restrictive ordinances or Zoning Codes. However, when designing the exterior of your house, two contradictory challenges will start to shape the design of your home:

- Your house CANNOT look like a carbon copy of every single home (or any home) in the neighborhood.
- Your house also needs to look like it belongs with the other homes and CANNOT look like it purposely does not belong or was dropped in from another time period.

Designing with the other buildings in mind is a conversation that does turn sour sometimes, with the same regularity of irritation as when Zoning or Building Codes dictate what people can or cannot do with their own property. Often for the same reasoning people say, "It's my property and I'll design and build whatever I want." I always sympathize with this frustration, but unfortunately, it's worth dwelling on. This is not an intentional dismissal from me, it's simply the harsh reality that you will not sway any Building Departments, Homeowners'

Associations or any Governing Authorities to your side with anger or irritation, so best to move forward.

I won't dwell on the legality of your design, as it has been covered in previous chapters. However, Zoning Codes often have language regarding what can or sometimes what MUST be used in the exterior design of your building. Luckily, you had an Architect do a preliminary Building and Zoning code review back in the Programming Phase to catch all these restrictions…and if you didn't then hopefully you made that mistake before reading this book. It's also worth mentioning that gated communities or wealthier neighborhoods that have Homeowners' Associations are very prestigious places to live and are often seem as desirable because of this. However, I can assure you that in all my projects these communities by far have the HARSHEST and most dictatorial regulations and guidelines and are even less forgiving in the appeals process than any government body.

But the design of your dream home is much more than just meeting Building and Zoning Codes, if it weren't then your dream home would be a large monolithic square with a door. There are countless factors that will begin to shape the design of your home, one of which will be covered in more detail in the preceding section. The one factor we are going to circle back to is the challenge of making your house unique but making it relevant to its neighboring buildings.

This concept may feel a little foreign, you may be desiring to create a one of a kind building that is clearly striking and is in harsh contrast to all others around it. Luckily an Architect can accomplish all those things WHILE designing it to be in context with its surroundings. Many clients who are spending the kind of money required to build their dream home are accepting that this will be their last home and they will be there until the day they die. They often ignore or don't even consider the concept of keeping the resale value in mind. I truly believe that when building a home, it should be built in a manner that it is going to be your house for the rest of your life. The number of shoddy, "throw away homes" being built is not only diminishing our built environment, but is costing the owners just as much as a much better quality product. It can't be ignored though that you won't be the last resident of any house built, as someday you will not be around.

You've probably seen the horror stories of estates or inherited homes that are beyond the size and value of anything in their zip code. Forcing the new owners to choose between carrying a huge financial burden in keeping a "white elephant" of a house, or offload the house at a cost that would make the previous owners turn in their graves. It must be said that being the biggest and priciest house on the block is great for your ego, but it's catastrophic for the value of your home, which only reinforces the importance of choosing an appropriate site in the initial stages. At times of economic strength land can be difficult to obtain, and many jump at the first parcel they can scavenge. Forcing them with too many compromises at later stages, after too much time and money has been invested. Your dream home should have NO compromises.

If the previous pages have started to sound as though designing your house can be a challenge, then I must apologize. There are many countless factors that must be considered in the design of your home, and while it is easy to view them as hinderances, this is the opposite to a design professional. I promised to avoid too much bashing of Contractors, but to an Architect a challenge is really an opportunity, whereas to a Builder a challenge is a "Change Order." (Term used for an increase in price or schedule is issued from the Contractor.)

During this examination of the neighborhood context, Zoning and Building Codes, resale value, and of course your requirements and requests, the building will begin to take shape. Some projects will also require periodic design reviews with the Authority Having Jurisdiction to confirm that your proposed building will be allowed. If this is the case then prepare for some additional time in the schedule, as a Building Official's schedule has no consideration of your own. This is also when your excitement level is going to be at its all-time high. Seeing your building's exterior design take form will start moving your dream home from your mind to seeing it in the real world.

Amidst all this excitement is a tendency for clients to focus on a lot of the same elements, while completely ignoring some other crucial components. Many times, the beginning phases of design are tough for clients as they spend a decent amount of time and money to not receive much information. I can't tell you how many times clients have sent me unpolite, or downright toxic, emails or phone calls expressing concern over an invoice I have sent and how "little" they perceive me completing on their project. Unfortunately, the beginning phases are a lot of work in terms of research, communication and coordination, and while the frustration of not having as many drawings to share with family and friends is understandable, this effort will GREATLY increase the success of your project. I won't harp on this too much right now, but if you want your project to be successful and stay on schedule, **PAY YOUR INVOICES.**

But after the frustrations of the project's beginning phases, you are now starting to see your building design take shape at this phase. As I mentioned before, this is the part where most clients focus on the number of windows shown, materials used on the siding, decorative elements of the porch, etc. These are all vital for your project's success, but there are other factors that should not be overlooked. In all my years of talking with clients though, I have yet to meet one who cared about the design of their roof and how the roof lines interact, nor has anyone shown concern over what kind of door thresholds are used at each door, and I can't imagine many Architects have had a client initiate the discussion of what termination detail to use where the Foundation Wall meets "Grade." (Term used for ground level of soil.) There is no pressure or expectation for you as the client to answer every question about your building, only to be prepared to review and discuss all the countless details you never considered as being relevant. You hired your Architect to be the expert who brings these unknowns to your attention.

At the conclusion of this part you will have your Building's Elevations, these are drawings that show each façade (side or face) of your house. These will not only show how your house looks, but will provide information on materials and finishes used, and the actual dimensions of your house. While it is tempting to start assuming your design is finished, it is important to keep your expectations clear, the next phase of Design Development is where your design is truly finished. To demonstrate what I mean by this, at Schematic Design you will have a clear idea on the number and sizes of your windows, however Design Development is where the actual product to be used will be determined.

# How Does Your House Interact with the Site?

It's unfortunate, but many people tend to design their homes as if they are floating in space, with no context of their surroundings. This building is then dropped down on a large enough piece of their site that will limit the amount of work needed. This is not a good approach, not even from the viewpoint of a Design Professional, but from the viewpoint of a pragmatic and efficient individual. You no doubt just said out loud to this page that you've seen homes built that way, and they have people living in them at this very moment. I won't argue with you that this has surely happened, but what you are not considering is how much money this wastes, not only with the initial investment at Construction, but with each subsequent Energy bill you would receive for the lifetime of your home.

If I were to ask people what the most expensive facet of New Construction is, the answers would vary, but most would probably focus on the structure of the house, which is not true. Structure is s large portion of your cost, but more money is dedicated to the "guts" of your house and on things you will never see; Electrical, Plumbing, Mechanical, etc. But usually the most expensive factor of Construction is the sitework preparation:

- Preparing new utility lines

- Getting access to local water and power

- Permitting and Clearances

- Regrading, the process of removing and adding soil to create the Topography needed for your design

It's a tough image for many clients to absorb, but a good chunk of money and time is going to be spent on "moving dirt around" and installing underground pipes and conduits you will never see in your life. I don't say all this to make jokes or make light of the situation, mainly to get your head wrapped around that now. I've watched quite a few people visit their sites during Construction, only to see a large field with no grass and become quite disturbed by the amount of money they had to spend to get a piece of land with a big hole in it, and nothing else visible to them. However, just as a House cannot stand without a proper foundation, a proper foundation cannot exist without sitework.

When hearing how much work is required to prepare a site for a project, is when many clients want to simply find the flattest spot of their site that is big enough for the house and work around that. It certainly can be argued that some money would be saved with this attitude, however it ignores all other factors, and at this phase is most when the entire site needs to be understood and designed accordingly. You may save money by not regrading the land at the house, but how far is it from the road? Unless you can teleport to your home, then you will need to have a driveway or road installed. Not only will distance affect the pricing of having a driveway or road poured, but if the grading you saved at the house is still spent getting the driveway or road ready, then you may not have saved anything.

You are also going to need utility lines buried underground to have access to water and power in the house. This part is a lot more costly than everyone assumes, but money aside, this part also requires a lot more planning and coordination than your wildest dreams. I can't speak for every Electric, Gas and Water provider in the country, but I do have experience with enough of them to warn you now that they work on their own schedule, make no exceptions for any of their requirements and will need to be brought into projects AS SOON as possible to keep your project on schedule. Again, if your home is just dropped on a flat portion of a site and ignores how this will affect the cost of getting utilities to it, then be prepared for some horrifying costs.

Something worth noting at this point is almost every one of these providers will want an "Easement" on your property in order to have access to their pipes and lines in the future. If you are unfamiliar with the term Easement, it is a portion of your property that others have special ownership of, in the terms of utilities it can be a path from the road to an access point for them, this section of your property CANNOT have any impeding structures or obstacles. So while you are expected to maintain that portion of "your" property, you cannot do anything that would prevent someone access to that section, and while it is your yard, they have permission to access it as if it were their own. I don't know of many people who do not become angry upon hearing that, but if you want water and power at your house, then it's a reality.

But moving forward, we will assume that you've found the perfect balance of the cost to have your site graded, driveway or road built, and utilities installed for the house. The potential cost and savings analysis are not solely limited to these items. The orientation and placement of your house itself can have an immense impact on your heating and cooling costs. There are many books in existence that fully explain the process of studying the effects that nature will have on your house, but how sunlight hits your home at certain times of the day will greatly impact your personal comfort and your heating and cooling bills and is worth discussing quickly here.

As you know, the sun rises in the East and sets in the West, with the sunlight being at its lowest angle when its rising and setting, thus shining more light directly into your eyesight. If your house has its kitchen sink with windows facing West, then after dinner when some unlucky soul must wash the dishes, they better be prepared to squint painfully as your windows allow direct sunlight to pierce into their eyes. The Southern façade of your home will get the most sunlight, particularly in Winter when the sun angle is at its lowest. While a South facing full glass wall at your living room would be amazing in an Elevation drawing, it would become unusable as it turns into an oven when more sunlight is brought in than anyone can tolerate.

In our modern age luckily, we have access to Air Conditioning and Central Heating. Because of this, whenever our interior environment becomes less than ideal, we can easily force it to be with a quick turn of a knob. However, if the same exact house was built twice, with two different orientations and the yearly cost to heat and cool them both were examined, there would be a significant difference between them. Placement of trees, water features, overhangs of your home and a million other things all need to be studied at this phase to give you your optimal performing home. Not only will it give you more to be proud of when others visit your new home, it will save you enough money with each energy bill to justify the cost of having this all explored at this Phase.

At the conclusion of this part you will have upgraded your initial Site Plan from Programming and Analysis to a full-fledged Site Plan, with the real footprint of your home and its true location and orientation on the site. This will also be your opportunity to flesh out any Site Elements to be constructed, including landscaping, hardscape, water features, tree lines, any countless other enhancements to your Dream Home. Do not forget, unless you plan to never leave your home or have any visitors, Design does not end with the interior, the exterior element is just as integral to your fully realized vision as everything else.

# Who Will Make Up Your Project Team?

This is the phase when you have fully committed to your Project Team. I would argue that this should have been accomplished during Programming and Analysis, however as we discussed, many clients are either pursuing that phase on their own accord or are trying to skip it altogether. Let me reiterate that you should NOT be doing either of those actions. Investigate thoroughly early or investigate these items at a much higher premium when others have more leverage.

I will stop you right there before you ask the next question, no this is not when you bring on your Contractor or Builder, that will occur during the Bidding Phase discussed much later. This is the creation of your project team of Consultants and Design Professionals who are involved in the Design and creation of Construction Drawings for your project. How many Consultants you will need to bring on is affected by the size, complexity and uniqueness of your project.

Throughout this book we are discussing your project in a traditional project delivery method known as "Design-Bid-Build," which is the method of having all your design work completed prior to having Contractors bid on the completed project. Later chapters will explain in further detail why this is the most effective method for you, the client. It is also a traditional method for the Owner to only hold two separate contracts, one with the Contractor and one with the Architect. In this scenario, the Contractor will be responsible for contracting and hiring all the necessary Sub-Contractors, and the Architect will handle Sub-Consultants. It's worth noting that the AIA (American Institute of Architects) have had the industry standard Contracts for the field of Design and Construction for over a hundred years, so often that is the best course of action for you to continue using them. It may seem biased to use a set of Contracts created by Architects, but they have been used, edited and debated in courts of disputes for over a century. It should go without saying that you will be wise to have your own lawyer review any contracts you sign with anybody though.

Regarding the Sub-Consultants, if you don't have a contact list of preferred Engineers and Consultants, then your Architect will have plenty they have worked with on a wide range of projects. If you DO have specific Consultants or Engineers you wish to bring on, that is a conversation to have with your Architect early on, particularly on whether you will hold those contracts or if they will contract with the Architect. It may feel as though you are giving up control, however holding fewer contracts as a client tends to be the simplest and most efficient project method. Holding a contract with your Contractor and your Architect and having them handle all their Sub-Contractors and Sub-Consultants makes more much quicker communication and simpler points of contacts and responsibilities. The more convoluted this web of "who is working for who" becomes, then there is greater chance of information not reaching all the relevant parties, not to mention schedule changes as conflicts begin to arise.

Once your project team is assembled, (cue the orchestral music) it is imperative to hold a kick-off meeting. This is one of the few times you will get everyone at the table at once. The field of Design and Construction is hectic, and juggling multiple projects are how many Consultant firms survive, so take advantage of this gathering. Not only will this meeting allow everyone to meet each other, but this is when multiple discussions that are vital to your project's success will need to be discussed amongst the entire team:

- Contact information and preferred method
- Project schedule and milestones of each party
- Any concerns or challenges that need to be addressed
- In-depth discussion of everyone's design and scope. If you think you are being too redundant or something is obvious, you are

not, and it isn't. I've seen projects have entire sections of a building be forgotten as it somehow slipped through the cracks, never leave any stone unturned

At the conclusion of this part, you will have your entire project team on board. There will also be a clear expectation as to what they are providing and at what point of the project they become involved in. Assuming you have followed the traditional contracting strategy of hiring an Architect who will then hire the Consultants, then your only contractual involvement is with the Architect. All communications will be directed to the Architect, who will then respond and coordinate with the other parties and will bring any matters to the client's attention that are relevant. If you just became concerned you may be missing some correspondence, the truth is you will eternally grateful for this filtering mechanism. At certain points in the project or Construction there could be hundreds of email threads and phone calls being bounced between parties in the course of a few days.

# <u>Conclusion of Schematic Design</u>

Now you've begun to see your dream home begin to materialize on the drawings of your project. It's a huge feeling of relief as you not only love the design, (speak up if you don't) but now it seems as though your project will be wrapping up and you can finally move on to Construction. That's how most clients start to react, you however have most likely noticed there are still three more phases before Construction in the Table of Contents and see this is not the end yet.

The good news is while your involvement as the client isn't over, your time commitment and stress levels will be greatly lowering at this point forward. (Until a rapid increase at the Construction Phase.) The next Phase, Design Development is where the Schematic Design is further tempered into a fully realized project, it's also where most of the Engineering is integrated into your house. Designing and placing all these Engineering systems will require some of your input, but it will also be a lot of work and research done behind the scenes from your Sub-Consultants and Project Team.

Your involvement will still be required, in fact Design Development cannot begin until you provide a formal "notice to proceed" to all parties.

This is the phase where your Architects and Consultants finalize all items and require less frequent discussion. Stay as involved as you like of course, but if you start feeling burnt out or stressed, feel free to lighten your load and let those of us that somehow enjoy this carry the load.

# Part Three:

Design Development

*10% – 20% of Architectural Fee*

In an attempt to "simplify" projects over the years, many have rolled Design Development into the same phase as Schematic Design. The erroneous assumption being that all design and technical decisions can be made at once, this has not proven to be the case though. While many times these phases are combined, that combination phase always seem to take MUCH longer than the two phases separated, so it's a simplification on name only.

The reasoning this is tough to achieve is rather obvious, it's much easier to make decisions when only factoring in a few items at a time. When presented with too many things to review, it becomes much harder to focus on an individual aspect. Consider the following two scenarios:

<u>Scenario One</u>

- Owner is first presented with only the layout of the home in terms of walls and built in casework only
- Once everyone agrees on the proper layout, the Project Team will move on to what furniture items should be in each room and discuss with Owner
- A conversation on what specific colors and finishes should be used is then had between the Project Team and Owner

- With all the information gathered, the Project Team begins to find the specific furniture items and paint colors, etc.

<u>Scenario Two</u>

- Fully completed drawings are sent to the owner, it includes final decisions on all furniture, casework, paint, layout and all items to the house.

- Owner is then expected to view every single element and approve or reject each individual piece based on all factors that need to be considered.

- The Project Team then replaces each rejected element with more elements, which are then sent to the owner to further accept or reject.

- Process continues until every item has been accepted by Owner and confirmed with Project Team.

Some are much more talented at multi-tasking then others, however I personally started getting anxiety when writing Scenario Two, as well as had some flashbacks to projects in the past that I've mistakenly agreed to combining the phases. This combination simply does not work, it will slowly get the design to take shape, but it takes a lot of frustrating reviews from the owner and tends to overwhelm most people. It may feel tedious, but it is beneficial to focus on things one phase at a time.

It's in this phase that the technical aspects of your home begin to become integrated with the Schematic Design portion. The amount of work and design that goes into providing your home with water, power and the ability to stay standing could fill multiple books. In this book however we are going to focus on the actual process of having these elements integrated from YOUR viewpoint.

If you are still wondering what is done in this phase that isn't delivered during Schematic Design, below are the questions that you will be focusing on and getting answers to during this phase:

1. How are you heating and cooling your home?
2. What fixtures, furniture and equipment will be in your home?
3. What is holding up your house?
4. What other documents will be included?

This is also where most of the Sub-Consultants "come alive" in your project. Their input is valuable in the Programming and Schematic phases; however, the design is so rudimentary at that point that there is not much they can offer at those stages. It often makes clients angry that many members of the Project Team have been "silent" up until this point, but it must be discussed that there isn't too much they can add until now. It can certainly be requested that everyone is always involved at every meeting and gathering, and I have indeed heard those who request it, but be warned that your invoicing and fees will drastically be raised, for not much more value.

# How Are You Heating and Cooling Your Home?

No matter how much research and innovative design you have placed into your home and its integration to the site, there will need to be some HVAC (Heating, Ventilation, Air Conditioning) system installed in your home. There have been some amazing strides in Passive Home Design over the years, and I will recommend how valuable it is to invest in your home at this stage. It's always tough to make this recommendation when many will focus instantly on the price tag, and yes it will cost more as an upfront investment to implement some innovation into your home. However, there are government programs to help lighten the load and there is the biggest motivator of all, much lower energy bills every month.

There are countless strategies to help increase your home's energy performance, and while occasionally you will run across a very new age "sci-fi" looking solution to be used in homes, you should never write off how simple it can be to implement energy efficiency into your dream home's design. Below are just a few design solutions that can easily be constructed by any Contractor or Builder: (If anyone tells you otherwise, then they are not equipped to build your home anyways.)

- Hyper Insulation in the walls

- Deeper roof overhangs

- Mass Walls, large stone or concrete walls that absorb sunlight and release it at night to help heat the colder space, as well as keeping a space cooler in the day after releasing any absorbed coolth. (Coolth is in fact a real word, it's the opposite of heat)

- Use of natural ventilation.

- Increased surface area of daylighting and windows.

- Thermal breaks in all walls and wall penetrations. (Prevention of heat transferring through building elements into the house)

These are a but a few of many other passive strategies that can be included in your home for a much lower cost than you probably envision. Often when discussing these with clients, it is usually brought up that I ignored Solar Panels and Windmills when discussing energy efficiency. I never mean to skip over them, it's just that these are considered "active" strategies and tend to cost much more than anyone will ever consider. If you are truly committed to building your dream home and living there to your last day, then investing in passive AND active energy strategies is priceless. If you truly feel you are unable to implement everything you can, then at the very least make the decision to include passive strategies into your home. A well-designed home and site can integrate passive design with very minimal cost difference, and if you need further convincing, even a minimal impact on your homes energy needs to save you greatly as your HVAC system is downgraded.

But even if you've collaborated and created an impressively energy efficient home, you will still need to consider an HVAC system. Our entire lives have conditioned us to always find the biggest version of anything and be happy with the fact that we are over covered with this conservative amount. Very often when buildings are being designed, the owner tends to think back to a poor performing house or building they occupied and have many negative memories of an underwhelming heater or air conditioner and instantly wants to put the largest industrial size system money can buy. Then taking comfort in the knowledge that nothing they could ever do could overload this new equipment.

First, the amount of money you just threw at that system could have given you a healthy budget to implement quite a few passive design strategies, which in turn would have allowed you to survive with a system a fraction of the size. Second, contrary to this comfort in knowing your system is much larger than needed, HVAC systems are their most efficient when they are running most of the time. This is hard for many to accept, as the notion of leaving things running instantly makes us regret their electricity cost, but when HVAC kicks on for a few minutes, blasts the house with cooling and then turns off again for a while, not only are you NOT saving electricity as the initial startup of these industrial systems is way more costly, but the air quality itself will begin to suffer. Air quality is something that nobody ever notices or cares about, until it's wrong, then it's the only thing anyone can notice.

While it is a great strategy to overcompensate in certain aspects of design, (never risk it when it comes to structural elements) HVAC is when you want to take your Engineer's advice and go with the appropriately sized system. Moving past the cost savings this will provide, many don't realize it until they begin the design process, but there is A LOT of things that happen above our heads in the ceilings. Unless you want your home to start becoming obnoxiously tall, then having an efficient system and ducts will prevent your floor levels from growing, or your ceiling heights to become uncomfortably short.

The number of factors that will need to be designed and considered cannot be covered in these pages. There is a reason each aspect of design has a designated Engineer for it. But an important conversation to have with your Architect or HVAC Engineer is HOW do you want your system to function? Do you want the whole house to be the same temperature or do you want each room to have its own temperature zone? The latter requires a lot of more ductwork and coordination in the ceilings. Do you live in a climate that only needs to either heat or cool the house in seasons? Or does it need to rapidly switch between both? Again, this is a special system that is required. I could throw a few hundred more rhetorical questions your way, but instead the point I am trying to make is HVAC is not simply a furnace with some ducts that need to be installed. It's a complicated portion of your design and you NEED to have in-depth conversations on what you need early on. Once these systems are installed, they can't usually be reused so have them figured out early or prepare to commit to whatever is installed.

At the conclusion of this part you will have your HVAC system specified, (more on that later) as well how your ductwork will be placed in your house. Some preliminary energy costs and performance data may also be available deepening on the systems you choose. If you do pursue any passive or active energy efficient strategies, (and I will keep harping that it's in your best interest to do so) then you can also have your Architect provide some daylighting models or graphics, as well as energy efficiency strategies.

# What Fixtures, Furniture and Equipment Will Be in Your Home?

Before we even dive into Programming and Analysis, many clients are already wanting to make decisions on what paint colors they want, what sink faucets they like, and other details we haven't reached yet. This is normal, and even understandable as we often build our mental homes out of elements we use or see in the world and commit to memory. These can certainly be discussed and considered in the earlier phases, but it isn't until this moment when it's time to put them into the design.

I often show clients Virtual Reality walkthroughs of their preliminary design, and in it I use placeholder sinks, furniture and other elements to make it look more like a residence. Quite often clients will focus on each of these elements and will react to them instead of the house itself, particularly the sink I use which never seems to be very popular. Just remember that in the beginning phases the design is focused more on the building itself. It's during Design Development when you truly are going to be talking about which faucet to use, what colors will be in the house, and infinitely more items.

Now picking your fixtures and equipment is not as simple as grabbing them off a manufacturer's website and having them put in a drawing.

Coordination with each of these elements needs to occur with the appropriate Engineers. The Plumbing Engineer needs to know every fixture they need to get water to and from. The Electrical Engineer will need to understand all the different elements of your house that will be pulling power. The HVAC Engineer will need to be aware that the hanging lights you want to use need to infringe on their duct space. The Structural Engineer will need to be aware of the Library you plan on putting in one of the rooms on the Second Floor. (Many don't realize this, but bookshelves are among the heaviest things in our buildings. That small library you have in your neighborhood has a beefier structural system than some parking garages.)

It is in this phase that you also need to confirm your selections against your project schedule. Your project still has a few phases left before completion, but at this point your project schedule has been established and needs to be considered. I cannot count how many times a very specific product is desired, only to find out during Construction that it takes months for it to be shipped to the site. At this phase you should have a handle on all the elements that will be included in your project, so it stands to reason that you should also be assured that nothing you want is going to throw your project off schedule.

At the conclusion of this part you will have made some significant strides towards your project's design. You will have most of the Finishes, Fixtures and Equipment for your home selected and specified. Most likely you will have an FF&E (Fixtures, Furniture and Equipment) Plan to help with your review of these selections. Nothing is set in stone of course; the next phase of Construction Documents will allow you to further confirm all your selections are appropriate and do not hinder any aspect of your project's design and success.

# What is Holding Up Your House?

Many people assume that all homes are wood framed construction and do not require any Structural Engineering effort. You probably already guessed that I disagree with this sentiment. It's true that if you stay beneath a certain square footage, there is a strong chance that your home will be wood framed and a lot of the detailing and Construction for that has been somewhat standardized over the years. However, when you start having a larger or more "unique" home built then you can very quickly enter the threshold of needing a Structural Engineer's expertise for your home's Construction.

Personally, any project I become involved in I heartily recommend a Structural Engineer; at the very least some time and effort for one to be involved in some capacity. (Even if it's an overview or review position.) At the end of the day, it doesn't matter how many years of experience ANYONE has, or how many projects they have successfully completed, all of that is irrelevant when it's YOU who is sleeping underneath some very "heavy" parts of your house. I know I would sleep easier knowing the building I put my life on the line every time I entered it was overseen and correctly designed by somebody who has proven their qualifications, expertise and knowledge.

It's also tough at times to review with clients the structural system in their home. It's not as exciting as the design drawings that can be shared with others. The vitalness of this system aside, it will impact almost every aspect of your home's design as well. It's far too common to focus on the aesthetics of your home and then try to shoehorn in a structural skeleton at the end. Your house can't stand without proper support, so it won't matter how ugly a column is if its interfering with all your windows. If it's determined at the end its needed, then it's going in, regardless of your irritation. This is where the value of integrating your structure early is invaluable to having a harmonious home. As I stated in the previous section, it won't be long before all the Engineers are fighting for your precious ceiling space and wall cavities. Structural elements tend to be the biggest consumers of these valuable spaces, but that can easily be dealt with WHEN you review all these elements early.

# <u>What Other Documents Will Be Included?</u>

There are few aspects of your project that you will opt to have little to no involvement whatsoever. One of them that you may decide is not where you would like to be involved in however, are the Project Specifications. Often referred to as the Project manual, (or the least interesting book you'll ever read) the Specifications are like the technical manual to the Construction of your house. Many assume Architects solely communicate in the language of drawings, however accompanying most drawings is a very large Project Manual.

One of the most jarring shocks to me when I ventured into the world of Residential Construction is very few projects are being built with any Specifications. This not only leaves a lot of information withheld when a project enters Construction, but it also leaves the Owners very vulnerable to Change Orders and cost overruns. A Specification is broken up into three sections:

- General
- Products
- Execution

A specification should be written for EVERY aspect of your project. Paint color, fasteners used for certain materials, roofing membrane used, siding for house, and hundreds of other items. Even a small home project could have dozens of Specifications, each one ranging from five to over fifty pages…that is a lot of information this Project Manual provides. Which is what is so terrifying about home projects being built without this vital information. What this leads to is assumptions being made by your Contractors, and assumptions are not a great way to do business when hundreds of thousands of YOUR dollars are on the line.

The chapter on the Construction Phase will delve deeper into some of the negative repercussions of a poorly written, or altogether missing, set of Specifications. But for now, it must be mentioned that no matter how thorough the drawings for your project are, they cannot come close to covering all the information necessary for a successful project. A simple Specification on drywall could cover over ten pages of information. (Unless your passion is drywall, these pages aren't the most riveting to read through either.)

Quick hypothetical situation for you to consider: a typical drywall Specification will go into detail how to patch and repair any damaged areas ruined during construction. If this Specification is missing and parts of your walls are damaged, without any specific language in the drawings stating the Contractor must patch and repair these damaged areas, the Contractor can either charge you to do so or flat out refuse the work. For any Contractors who just rolled their eyes or even became angry, I have Change Orders from past projects in other firms to prove this is an issue arising from projects without Specifications.

A well-documented project will format the drawings to refer those reviewing them to the Specifications. The drawings provide a graphic explanation of the work, and the Specifications provide all the legal and technical information required for aspects of the work. The two must work in tandem, and if the Specifications are removed to save money, (which it won't) then the drawings must now pull double duty to cover all the information, and sadly that won't happen. As the sub heading states however, these are not particularly enjoyable to read through, as a few hundred pages dedicated to things such as which national standard to use when measuring the moisture content of your wood studs is boring for most individuals. However, the importance of these documents cannot be overlooked for their role in keeping your project on budget during Construction.

At the conclusion of this part you will have a draft of your Project Specifications. While most of the research and effort can be put into having these almost finished, there inevitably will be changes and edits made during the Construction Documents Phase.

<u>Conclusion of Design Development</u>

It is at this point that your design should be done, time to rejoice! However, the completion of your design is not the completion of your project. You now need to have drawings completed to convey this design to the Contractors that are going to bid on your project. These documents will not only need to explain the design, but clearly state how this design needs to be constructed… no small task. Luckily the effort expended in this phase, and all the others previous, will make it much easier to complete the Construction Documents.

Just as many who force Design Development to share a seat with Schematic Design, often I see Design Development rolled right into the Construction Documents phase. Again, this is a mistake as it will only overwhelm and cost more money. Design Development is the selection of all elements and finalizing all Engineering required to make your dream home a reality, whereas Construction Documents is where it is explained how this is all to be built.

# Part Four:

Construction Documents

*25% – 35% of Architectural Fee*

The Construction Documents Phase is a bit of a mystery for some clients. It's at this phase that the design is fully realized and practically finished, and yet the creation of the Construction and Permit Drawings is the largest phase by far (excluding Construction) in terms of the time needed from the Architect and the Project Team to complete. This confusion is furthered by the fact that besides any last-minute discussions, your involvement as a client is limited at this point.

While that uneasiness is understandable, this is the phase when your Architect and their team apply their expertise and knowledgebase in finishing your home. Despite the limited involvement necessary, I strongly urge you to take this time to learn everything you can about your project and the documents. You may be building again in the future, hopefully not your home if you went with the right team this time. Or you may find another who is as lost with the whole process as you were before we took this journey together. Being able to pass on everything you have learned will be an invaluable contribution to their project's success as well.

In your attempt to help anyone though, make sure you remember that this design and the drawings themselves are not freely permissible to give away. There is nothing wrong with letting others admire your future design or even take away elements they are envious of. There is a problem however with giving them a copy so they can find somebody to go build it for them. I've gone into detail on design copyrights earlier, but in the next section we will also examine that a drawing without a stamp is technically "useless" and wouldn't be usable for anyone to build anyways…This of course is not stopping some Builders or Contractors from building without a legal set of drawings. I hope for your sake though if somebody was willing to break the law, then you hopefully aren't going to be comfortable handing them a few hundred thousand dollars and trusting them with your dream home.

I also must advise against those who want to save money and use these drawings to get some aspects done by themselves, or even worse a local handyman who claims to know how to build things. Often people discuss with me their intent to save on the cost of their project and do the painting themselves or have a friend of theirs installing the kitchen cabinets, and a whole assortment of other tasks to save money. I personally made the mistake of building a pantry myself in my home for my wife, and it was only a few short days before we placed a large view obscuring DVD shelf in front of it. Best intentions are always at the forefront of a mistake, and that is exactly what it is to have ANYTHING done by someone who is not a professional.

For all the frustration I have occasionally expressed at some lies and misleading done by Contractors, the reality is they are the Construction Professionals. If you have spent all the money hiring professionals to design your project, its only foolish to try and save money on the people who are going to be building it. If I sound a bit too harsh on the "friend" or the "handyman" people often try to bring into the project, it's because I've seen too many of their mistakes in my career. Almost every home I have been hired to renovate or inspect ALWAYS have some low-quality work done, in some cases done so poorly that damage was done, and it's always the items they had some "handyman" work on to save money. I will say the same thing for Contractors, Architects and anybody else you want to hire…**If they don't believe in their craft enough to have set up a business, then they are not ready OR capable enough for your project.**

There is some pressure at this point in the project though. In all the previous chapters, I kept telling you that there is time to fine tune your selections and decisions related to your home. Here however, is where it's time to commit and be ready to say it's "perfect." I apologize for the quotation marks, but I've never seen a home keep the same furniture or paint color after a few years, its only human nature to keep editing our living spaces. I don't want to pile it on too thick, but here is the last chance to make changes that won't have impacts on the Project

Schedule or cost. If you and your Architect have stayed in contact and have had regular communications, then there should be no worries. However, we will go into why you won't want to make any unnecessary changes past this point in the later chapters.

As you enter this phase its only normal to begin fixating on the finish line and gaining tunnel vision, after all this time of seeing your fantasy home become a reality is naturally exciting. You need to focus however, there is still a lot of coordination and fine tuning necessary to take your Schematic drawings and renderings and turn them into a feasible Construction project. The questions you will be focusing your attention at this point are below:

1.  What are stamped drawings and who is providing them?
2.  Who handles the Building Permit?
3.  How is you house actually built?
4.  Is your budget still realistic?

# <u>What Are Stamped Drawings and Who is Providing Them?</u>

When you begin discussing your project with your Architect the term "Stamped Drawings" will begin to be thrown around occasionally. Whenever an Architect or Engineer earn their Professional License, they are entered into a public database, and are given an official Seal through their state. This Seal contains their name, license information and the state they are licensed to practice in. A Stamped set of drawings is an official drawing set that has been stamped by the overseeing Architect, or Engineer over their own drawings.

Quick note, an Architect licensed in one state cannot perform work in another state, they can file and prove their capability to practice in other states, however. Many Architects and Engineers will begin amassing a collection of stamps for different states they work in. If your preferred Architect or Engineer is not in your state, that isn't an issue, they can become licensed in your state and still perform the work. What CANNOT happen, and sadly is a conversation I have often, is having an Architect or Engineer perform work, and then ask a local Architect or Engineer to sign off on it. Not only is it illegal to stamp a drawing that you have not had "Responsible Control" over, but if someone isn't committed or confident enough to get licensed in a project's state, then the work they did is most likely unacceptable. These Professional stamps are not simply us stating "we approve of these drawings," they are also us providing our information in case anything goes wrong and we must accept liability and even defend what happens in court.

If your project has other Consultants involved, then they are responsible for the drawings necessary for their scope of work. Architects know a lot of things from various trades and Engineering disciplines, but they won't have the specific expertise in each of the relevant aspects of your home. Many "simpler" homes below a certain size tend to skip the use of a Structural Engineer when having their home built, or many of the other Engineers as well. I will always preach the necessity of hiring the right professionals for your home, as an Engineer who places their professional liability and reputation on the line with their designs tend to be more thorough than a Contractor who risks neither.

At the conclusion of this part, you will have your stamped Construction Drawings. A stamped set is often the "final" set of drawings. When Permit Drawings are issued, or Construction Documents are issued, an Architect's stamp is required for them to be used by others. Because of the importance and severity of putting our stamp on a drawing, many (including myself) will never send an electronic set of drawings with this stamp on it. Living in the digital age, I understand my client's frustration with this as it comes up. However, many Architects have had someone send an official set of drawings to others, and this set has been used for purposes not agreed to by everyone. It has also never been easier to take or edit anything digitally, and an Architect or Engineer's stamp can be manipulated to do some scary things. You most likely have already gathered some Floor Plans and drawings you like for your new house, and that is perfectly acceptable. Understand that without any of them being stamped, they are just reference materials and not usable documents…If any of them do have stamps, then quickly return them to wherever you got them, and we will move on to getting a Building Permit for your project.

<u>**Who Handles the Building Permit?**</u>

Your project will need to have drawings submitted to the Authority Having Jurisdiction and a Building Permit approved before Construction can begin. I'm always asked if a Building Permit is required, and I always have the same answer, "We will assume it is and reach out to the Building Department." Every municipality is different, and during Programming and Analysis is when you will have your Architect get a clearer picture of what they are dealing with. However, below are a few general rules of thumb regarding when a Building Permit is required:

- If your building footprint is changed, whether its size changes or its shape changes, then you will need one.

- If you are building a new building, then you will need one.

- If any Interior walls are being added or removed, then you may need one.

- If any portions of your house being constructed do not meet any current Energy, Accessibility or Building Codes, then you will need one. As well as proving it will meet these codes.

- If any hazardous material will be disrupted or removed from your project, then you will need one. When Asbestos is involved you will also need a certified Asbestos Project Designer and Certified Construction Handler for this work, believe me when I say the penalty fees are not worth risking it.

- If a Competing Contractor who did not win the job becomes angry, then you'll need one. As well as you will need to disprove any of the outrageous claims made to the Building Department.

That last one may have made you chuckle, or rolled your eyes in disbelief, however you reacted its certainly happened though. Whether you think one is needed or not, it's always a good course of action to speak with your Building Department. If you took my advice from earlier, then you should have been speaking with them from the beginning. I could fill a separate book with all the last-minute surprises some clients have had from their local building department, none of which you want for your project. This early communication will also have the added benefit of keeping your project on track. The Building Department and their Officials' schedules will rarely align with yours, and the sad truth is they may become overwhelmed with "higher priority" projects than your home. Your dream house is the most important thing in your world, but sadly it is often nowhere near as urgent to them as many other projects. Speaking with them early on will give you a chance to get some honest feedback on how much time they need and when the best time for them to review anything is. It's very important to recognize I used the term "review" instead of "approve." I can count on one hand the number of times a project was simply submitted and then approval was granted…there is often questions that need to be addressed before approval is granted. It should go without saying that your project can't begin Construction until this approval is granted, so no matter how trivial or irritating their comments are, you will need to address them fully.

People are often given conflicting information on who handles the Building Permit process itself, is it the Contractor or the Architect? Assuming you are following the project method of "Design – Bid – Build" that I have been trying to demonstrate in this book as the most beneficial to you as the client, then the Architect will be who handles the Building Permit, as the Contractor is not on board yet. This is also a lot easier for your Architect as they not only have been communicating with the Building Department from the start, but chances are they have worked on quite a few projects with this same department before and familiarity can only help alleviate this process.

It's better to hire an Architect to have your design fully finished very early, even before you may be considering Construction. This will prevent any stressing over the schedule and will allow you the freedom to begin your project at the best possible time for you. Many clients I speak to assume they can't start with Design until they are ready to fully commit from start to finish and have the project built as well, this is not true. A completed project design can be held and used later. The only time pressure given is the fact that the Building Code and Accessibility guidelines are updated every three years, so if you stay within that window you should be fine. If not, then it will be revisited to confirm all new codes and guidelines are met.

Residential projects tend to move on a much faster pace, however. In other firms I have worked on projects that have taken years to finish and were not built for a few years later. Your Building Permit, however, is not a lifetime approval. Every municipality is different, but commonly these permits are valid for a year. Extensions certainly can be appealed for, but it's often not worth it. Design can be done as early as you want but applying for your Building Permit and having the Construction started does require you to be ready once you go down that path.

At the conclusion of this part, you will have your approved Building Permit for Construction. I hope it isn't necessary to make this case, but I have been brought onboard with too many projects where the clients needed to hear this earlier, so here goes…NEVER TRY TO BUILD WITHOUT A PERMIT. If you think you can hide it, you can't. People are out there dedicated to finding these illegal projects. It only takes one time for a Contractor's van or truck with their logo to pull into your driveway before somebody is notified. It also only takes one Construction accident for the Building Department to be notified, and any cost savings you thought you achieved by trying to hide it have not only been removed, but so has any goodwill or patience the Officials will have for you and your home. If you think the Builder or Contractor who advised you a Permit wasn't needed is going to help you out in this situation, then you will be in for a rude awakening.

<u>How is Your House Actually Built?</u>

The Construction Documents are not just the drawings showing your completed design, they are the graphic instruction manual to how your house is going to be constructed. In fact, they are not only the drawings for your project, they are also the Technical Specifications, hence why they are referred to as "Construction DOCUMENTS," not Construction Drawings. What many don't realize though, is these Construction Documents are not just a set of drawings and a large Specifications book, they are part of the contract between Owner and Contractor. This will be explored in further detail in the following chapters, but when a Contractor submits their bid, it is based solely on what is shown in the drawings and Specifications. (Further proof of the necessity of Specifications.) I don't say all this to stress you out but considering how often clients want to rush into Construction, I must make it clear on why the time and effort needs to be expended here.

In this same vein, I often see the mentality that only the broad scope of a project needs to be covered, and all the micro level details can be figured out later. This can certainly be achieved, but it's going to cost YOU significantly more for each item left open to interpretation at this point. A quick example of this will help demonstrate my point. If you know you want a large glass window in one room, but you are not sure of the size or product to be used, you may think that a price can be applied to the fact that you want a large window. A price will be applied, but in order to cover any cost on their end, the Contractor is going to price you at the highest possible price imaginable for this element.

Even when presented with "easier" choices to be made, the price will never end in your favor. If another location needs a decision between two doors, one being made of wood and the other being made of glass, The Contractor is forced to price the more expensive option. (Glass) But since they know some time will be spent having a discussion with the client over it, then some additional cost will be added…so you not only paid for the higher costing item, but you actually paid a higher premium on it. Unless you have a very in-depth line by line estimate for the project as well, you aren't going to catch this cost increase, nor will you be given any money back if you end up with the cheaper option. This is only for one element of your house, when this starts happening with the hundreds of pieces assembling your home, some serious money is going to be thrown away. Case in point, every question a Contractor must ask when looking at your drawings is going to cost you much more than having a definitive answer. This is the reason you are hiring an Architect to prepare these Construction Documents.

<u>**Is Your Budget Still Realistic?**</u>

This section could have been placed as the last part of all the previous phases. However, to avoid the redundancy that would cause, or the viewpoint of me padding out this book's length, we will simply cover it in depth at this point. Throughout your project you will be getting feedback from a Cost Estimator on what your project should cost when it comes time for the Bidding Phase. If your Project Team has been doing their due diligence and the Cost Estimator has been regularly reviewing the project, then you should have very few surprises.

Having said that, if you add any big project elements or make any large-scale changes, prepare for a significant change in the cost estimate. If these changes must occur, then make them at the earlier phases of Schematic Design or Design Development, NOT NOW. Adding a two story, all glass swimming pool would make you the envy of all your neighbors, but it will be a waste of your Architect's time and money to create the Construction Details and write Specifications for this, only to find out it is significantly out of your budget.

It's never a fun conversation to have with clients, but the world's greatest Cost Estimator could be reviewing the most complete set of

Construction Documents ever created, and sadly when it comes time for the Bidding Phase an unexpected external factor can throw a wrench into all cost bids and proposed schedules that Contractors will submit. After months of working on and detailing a set of Construction Drawings for a local government agency, a political situation across the world (that nobody could have predicted) caused an immense shortage of structural steel…causing all the bids for this small project to be roughly 20x more costly and over six months longer due to the steel's lead time. The disappointment felt by the client when this happened is a memory I can vividly recall after all these years. This presents the perfect opportunity on the value of designing and creating your home out of more readily available materials and products. I am not proposing for a moment to compromise and pick solely on cost, but sometimes it's better to build a custom shelving unit in your Master Bedroom Closet then ordering an obscure product from across the world.

A Cost Estimator is your best resource for cost data; however, they shouldn't be the only source of information you tap into. Coordinating with manufacturers of the products, materials and systems you plan to use is something that EVERY Architect should be doing during your project. The amount of information they can provide on that one aspect of your project will often be enlightening. Not to mention, no Architect,

Contractor or Cost Estimator can know the lead times, costs and details needed for every single product on the planet, necessitating the need to speak with these representatives. Necessity aside, many people forget that a salesperson is paid based on sales and tend to ignore or exaggerate the truth. I hate to burst anyone's bubble, but often clients have begun talking to these sales representatives prior to engaging an Architect, which is perfectly fine, but become disappointed when I as the Architect am told something very different than what they were told.

At the conclusion of this part, you will have your most accurate Cost Estimate. At this point it will be a much more in-depth estimate that will allow you to get a true understanding of your project cost and where those costs are associated. In fact, your budget should be comfortable enough to cover all your costs and have some healthy surplus. It's human nature at this point to see this extra money as potential for improving your project with more square footage or better elements. As much as some Architect love projects with increased scope and cost, you really need to avoid this temptation. If you've been following my framework, then you should have had your dream home fully realized already, and that extra money can always be used in the future. If you spent significant time and money on your beautiful home, then adding more "tassels" and decorations won't improve the quality you've worked for.

<u>Conclusion of Construction Documents</u>

Your project is done! It's fully designed, all your unknowns and concerns have been addressed and its perfect. You show it off to all your friends and family and now your even more excited and anxious, as you can't wait to move into this dream home made reality. This is often when an intense mixture of emotions occurs for clients:

- Relief that your project is finally finished.
- Excitement at the design turning out better than imagined.
- Irritation that all you have is a large set of drawings.
- Impatience of wanting it built right now so you can move in.

I will avoid making a blanket statement that the project is done with design, things always come up. But I will express as hard as I can with this sentence, it's now time to stop designing and tinkering. You will have plenty to stress about in the coming phases. Ominous foreshadowing, I know, but stick with me and you'll feel more confident to handle what is about to come.

The next two phases, Bidding and Construction Administration, vary greatly from the previous phases as they are solely "reactive," while the earlier phases are "proactive." To put this simpler, during the initial design phases, communication is held between all parties and all coordination and design is completed before they are necessary. During Bidding and Construction Administration, all communication and effort required from the Project Team is mostly reacting to issues or items raised by the Contractor. Often these items will have cost and schedule impacts, which only increase the necessity of a fast and efficient response. It also must be said that decades of Construction culture have unfortunately engrained in most Contractors the mentality that every question or item to be discussed is an emergency or "project threatening" dilemma. This is often not the case and you will be grateful to have an Architect on your side defending you from these exaggerated claims. If you don't have an Architect, however, prepare for a lot of extra costs and unnecessary services.

# Part Five:

Bidding

*5% of Architectural Fee*

Now that a pretty significant amount of time has passed since you began the Programming and Analysis Phase, it's time to bring a Contractor on board. This may seem like a radical shift in how projects are usually run, as many people have either been told to hire a Contractor early, or they themselves have hired a Contractor first. (Then occasionally brought others in as it was legally required.) This is why it's shocking to most clients that the Residential world of Design and Construction is the only time this happens, whereas barring a few exceptions, almost all other project types follow the "Design – Bid – Build" project delivery method we have been discussing.

But is must be noted that this phase is referred to as "Bidding," not "Hiring A Contractor." This is because at the completion of Construction Drawings you are not going to just hand them to a single Builder. Instead you are going to ask a few Contractors to review the Construction Documents and submit a bid outlining what they will charge you to complete the project and what schedule they would propose. This goes against how most clients go about the process of reaching out to a Contractor. I've seen many clients contact a Builder or Contractor and, attempting to expedite the process, they simply inform the Contractor of their budget and schedule and want to know if it can be completed. I understand the reasoning behind this method, but unfortunately a phenomenon known as "Parkinson's Law" takes effect. (The concept that regardless of how much time is needed to complete a task, when given more time, the task will still take the whole time allotted.) The Contractor's fee and time will match both numbers you have asked them about, even if their true projections were much lower. This assumes of course that you weren't unreasonably low in either, in which case they will gladly share that with you.

How many Contractors you want to bid will depend on the project. For Residential Construction though, a good range is between three to five Contractors. Anything less than three and the perception of not having any competition will cause the prices to skyrocket. Anything more than five and you will have an overwhelming amount of communication during Bidding, as well as many feeling as though they won't have a chance and therefore not put as much effort into their bids.

Now, there is no denying that having multiple Contractors bidding will give you a better price. But as this is your dream home you do need to thoroughly review each bid and NOT focus on cost only. If you skip right to the last page and choose whoever had the lowest number, you will increase your risk of a poorly done project. You are certainly looking for the best price, but you need to review all the factors:

- Schedule

- Experience

- Average amount of change orders in projects

- Insurance / Bonding (We will review later)

- **THOROUGH UNDERSTANDING OF ALL THE CONSTRUCTION DOCUMENTS.**

That last one is a hot topic for me. When a Contractor submits a bid on your project, they are committing that their price and schedule covers ALL items in the Construction Documents. Now, if the Contractor does miss things, even though they have committed that their bid covers everything, I have NEVER seen a Contractor who didn't try to get paid for items they should have already priced you for. If you receive four bids for a project with three of them ranging from $190,000 - $250,000 and one bid for $110,000 your first reaction will be "What a great price!" But you need to step back and realize that they clearly missed a few things the others did not. If you decide to go with them, then it will only be a few days before they start trying to recover all their misplaced bid money from you, contract or not. This will only be worse as after a contract is signed and Construction begins, your Contractor gains a lot more leverage, so you really need to have backed the right horse.

While the Contractors bidding on your project will have their fair share of questions, you will have your own questions to worry about. The questions you are looking to answer at this stage are as follows:

- What can you live without and what would you like?
- How do you handle questions?
- How do you protect yourself from risk?
- How are bids received?

<u>**What Can You Live Without and What Would You Like?**</u>

Before your Construction Documents are completed and sent to your potential bidders however, there is one more conversation you need to have with your Architect. As much as I have been spouting to stop designing and to keep yourself content with your project as is, it's hard to fight your innate need to consider other options and to add as much as possible to your dream home. You have the option for your bids to cover a few different scenarios. These are known as "Alternates" and they can be additive or deductive.

There are a few terms that are going to be used in almost every email or phone call sent during this phase, and it's vital to your Project's success that you become familiar with them. Don't fret, your Architect will be handling all communications and coordination items, however chances are you are not going to be content just sitting back and letting it all be handled behind the scenes. There is also a strong chance that many Contractors and Sub-Contractors will be copying you on every email they send, REGARDLESS of whatever communications protocols you all agreed to. This tends to be the number one cause of Owner stress when projects enter Construction.

It's only natural that when you open your email and see thirty something emails regarding an issue that needs to be corrected or is hindering someone, you begin to feel panicked and think the project is going off the rails...A project I completed which only involved converting an existing Garage had hundreds of communications between parties, THIS IS NORMAL. Take a deep breath and only panic when your Architect is panicking.

When you are having your Construction Documents completed you have the ability to include items you are not sure you have the budget for. These are "Additive Alternates." The logic for these is simple, you may ask for a bid to construct your home, and you may also ask for a price for that same home but with an addition of an all glass conservatory attached to one of the rooms. The Contractors will then submit their "Base Bid," (price to construct the home) and then a separate cost to build that Alternate Conservatory. What this presents to you is the ability to have them continue with the house and disregard the Conservatory if it's out of your budget, or to continue with both if they end up being affordable.

The other method to consider is an "Deductive Alternate," which is the opposite of an Additive Alternate, the logic being you ask for a Base Bid of having the previously mentioned home built WITH the Conservatory, and then a separate price to have the Conservatory portion removed from the project. At first glance you may have not seen the difference between the two, simply a change in wording, however depending on your situation one is often more advantageous.

Often the Deductive Alternate method gives you better pricing. There are always exceptions, but if you are considering this route of seeing how much you can add to your project, I always advocate for putting as much in as possible and then getting a price to deduct it. A large cost of Construction is simply having the Contractor and their forces "mobilize" and get set up at your site. Whether you are building a 100 square foot shed or a 1000 square foot shed, the cost will not be as different as you might imagine as the same amount of permitting, travel and set up must be done for that tiny shed.

This same reasoning can be applied to Bidding, the best price you will get for a project is at the initial start when they want to win the job, so if you have everything included then you will find they really won't offer much financial incentive in deducting any of the elements. Be warned however, every item of your project has a percentage applied for profit, and even if items are deducted the profit is never removed. While it's tempting to stuff your project with every add on you can think of, when you are forced to start cutting them out for budget, then you are gifting quite a bit of profit to the Contractor or Builder.

Conversely, when Construction has begun or when reviewing Bids, anything being added to your project is going to cost significantly more. At this point you no longer just pay the purchase price for anything, you pay an inflated labor cost, cost for communication time, and generally just a cost for the fact that the Contractor has all the leverage. I hate to come off like a pessimist, but it's truly best to enter Bidding and Construction with the mentality that you CANNOT add anything, or if you do then prepare to pay an insulting premium.

Not too many pages previously, I had strongly urged you to avoid tacking on more things because you perceive more money is available. I am not condoning the idea of inflating your project to an unreasonable size with the use of Alternates. If you include too many or too confusing of Alternate bid packages, then that confusion or extra work will directly translate into increased bid prices. I always recommend to either avoid them completely or to just stick with ONE, don't get greedy.

At the conclusion of this part, you will have your Construction Documents and all Alternate Bid Packages. It's finally time to send them to your interested parties and see what it's going to cost and how long it's going to take. (Fingers crossed)

<u>How do You Handle Questions?</u>

There is a significant chance that your bidding Contractors are going to have questions for you when preparing their Bids. Let's not mince words here, they are going to bombard you and your Architect with a ton of questions, suggestions and clarifications needed. I am always amazed that some clients don't have an Architect representing them during Bidding and Construction, not only from a protection standpoint, but from the mere fact that it takes dedication to try and coordinate all the communication blasts they are about to receive.

This phase mostly consists of the Contractors and Architect exchanging RFIs and the corresponding Addendums. You most likely weren't sure what I was referring to in that sentence, and if you were then you have given yourself away as someone in the Construction field giving this book a critical review. (Thanks for sticking with me so far.) At the conclusion of this part, and after all the back and forth communication, you will have your submitted and VALID bids to select a Contractor.

An RFI is a "Request for Information," and these will be submitted from the Contractor or their proposed Sub-Contractors. These could be a range of many items they are inquiring about:

- Something in the Construction Documents was unclear.

- They have a suggestion they want to run by you.

- They want to propose a substitution for a material or product.

- Anything else that will affect their price.

An Addendum is any official change to the Construction Documents, and they are issued by the Architect and are issued to ALL BIDDERS at the same time. If any answers or items were submitted to one bidder and not the others, then an unfair advantage has been given and will cause more than a few cases of anger.

As involved as you want to be, you need to stick with your agreed upon communication protocols. It will save you a lot of time, confusion and irritation. I always recommend letting a few RFIs come in, and at weekly or twice weekly intervals having the Architect send out an Addendum containing all answers. It also must be stated that any changes to the Construction Documents made need to be done in a way that is OBVIOUS to anyone looking at it. There is nothing worse than showing up at a Construction Site and everyone gathering around an outdated set of documents and trying to blame you for the fact that they didn't keep up with communications. Addendums can be a wide range of formats for responses:

- Written responses.

- New or edited Construction details.

- Adding or deleting sections of the Specifications.

- Anything else needed to provide a NON-VERBAL response to any issues or questions raised.

It's imperative that a few deadlines be set during Bidding. First, set a deadline for when all RFIs must be received, as well as a deadline for when your Architect needs to issue their Addendum. This forces the Contractors to review the project early; instead of the usual last-minute "fire drills" they are familiar with, resulting in a lot of late-night emergency emails. You will also want to set a deadline for when Bids must be received, every project is different, but 2-3 weeks is standard. This could last indefinitely if you don't put a cap on it. I also must constantly push clients to be firm with their deadlines. It may seem spiteful to disqualify a Contractor who submits their bid late, but if they couldn't even handle looking at the Construction Documents in a timely manner, how can they be expected to build the actual structure on time?

To say that you are vulnerable during the Construction phase is an understatement. Luckily, there are measures that can be taken to minimize this risk. You are going to find opposition to everything I discuss in this section. I don't know how, but many Contractors have been completing projects without any of these measures in place. It boggles my mind to no end how anyone could ever agree to moving a project forward with absolutely no protection for themselves, except for the obvious reason that they haven't been informed otherwise.

When you begin choosing Contractors to bid on your project, you are going to need to engage much more than the minimum number I have suggested. The reason is many are going to either debate or refuse many of the protective measures I am going to suggest shortly. Those were not the Contractors you wanted anyways, they will always give you a list of twenty or more references to call. But when things go sideways, those positive referrals won't mean a thing when you get stuck with some very harrowing and costly problems.

Despite any harsh conversations had, at the conclusion of this part you will have some contractual protection from Contractors bidding on your project. These measures will help protect you financially if the project is not completed and protect you legally if any accidents or issues arise on the Construction Site. It may also feel frustrating at first, but the weeding out of anyone unwilling to offer you protection is the biggest advantage I can think of, it makes me shudder to think what could have happened if you became locked into a contract with them.

The first thing you are going to require your Bidders to submit is proof of insurance AND Bonding capabilities. Talk with you Architect on which bonds your project will need the Contractor to carry. Bonds are simply Surety (Insurance) companies that will provide guarantees that if the Contractor fails certain tasks, (Completing, Labor and Materials, etc.) then they will pay you the money needed to have another Contractor finish without you losing all the money you have spent so far. Many will fight this; I've heard every version of the statement "this is unnecessary and will cost the client too much money, just skip it" from Contractors I bring this up to.

What that means is they either are unable to get a Bond from one of these sureties, in which case they are the LAST people you want to hire, or they are trying to squeeze every penny of profit they can get and don't want to pay the fee required to carry this. The MEAGER cost of a Bond is infinitely more valuable than the hundreds of thousands of dollars you could lose if the Contractor goes bankrupt or disappears. If that sounds dramatic, it happens far too often.

Many measures of protection you will need will fall under the category of money and payment items. We will dive into more detail for these items in the next Phase, but they are all items you will need to have confirmed at the Bidding phase:

- Agreement to having Architect involved with invoice review.
- Retainage provisions in invoice payment.
- Release of Liens and Affidavits at project completion.
- Payment WILL NOT be in cash. (Get as far away as possible from anyone who even suggests this)

Many of these items will garner pushback, if so then you do not want to work with them anyways. They may get creative in the reasoning why they won't provide these items in their bids, but it will always center around the truth that all these items put more pressure on them for a successful project. While it is easy for Contractors to tell you YOUR risk aversion and protection is not valuable, I imagine when it comes to your home and your finances, both are priceless.

The moment of truth has arrived, the prices are in! In the Residential world, there is not as much of a formal proceeding for this as there is in the public sector. However, I often try to mimic the public sector even for homes as there is a lot about it that would benefit Homeowners immensely. For one thing, the bids should be read anonymously. No matter how hard you try you will have become in contact with the different Contractors and they no doubt have colored your perception, either positively or negatively, when reviewing the bids it's best for you to try and remove this initial bias you most likely gained.

After reviewing your bids and at the conclusion of this part you will select the "Lowest Bona Fide Bid," a term to describe the bid that the lowest price AND covered all the necessary scope, you will then notify your Contractor and have a final meeting to discuss any last minute items and to sign the Contract between you two. The AIA does offer a full suite of Contracts to use between you as the Owner and the Contractor. I've already made my case on the ease and value of these contracts, however you will no doubt need to involve your lawyer at this point. If you are considering saving money and not hiring a lawyer, then first of all I have failed in all my previous pages of convincing you the value of the right Professionals, but secondly I ask you to reach out to me or do an internet search and see all the horrific stories of people losing everything because of a bad or MISSING contract.

What I am going to say next will no doubt offend quite a few...Do NOT approach this with intent for negotiation. When you begin asking for bids you are going to find quite a few Contractors who will not be thrilled with the idea, as they will be fearful that you are going to use their bid to shop around for cheaper prices, and many are justified in their paranoia as this somehow has become commonplace. I understand the desire for the lowest price possible, but doing this will not get you that, it will simply lead you down a road to failure. If your current supervisor told you they need you to continue your job with a 10% salary reduction you will react in one of two ways: complete anger and refusal to do so, or complete anger and with much reduced effort and begin looking elsewhere. Do either of those responses sound like the person you want building your dream home?

No doubt you also considered shopping around for your Architect as well, you may have even scoffed at the initial pricing I explained at the very beginning of this book. For some reasons unknown to me, the Residential world seems to have a rampant case of people shopping around for prices among Architects. If you use one Architect's proposal to shop around for a cheaper one, you may find someone who will agree to that price. When you enter into this arrangement however, you are dooming your project's success. An Architect's price is derived from the amount of time they must spend to make your project succeed. If you lower that fee, you are lowering the time they can spend on it. If they run out of hours for your project, then they need to move on to the next one. This may infuriate some, but bills cannot be paid by telling a collector you are working on a project for an owner who didn't respect you enough to pay the full amount. Either accept or reject a Contractor's (or Architect's) proposal, do not sour communication by trying to haggle. **THIS IS YOUR DREAM HOME, NOT A LAMP YOU FOUND AT A GARAGE SALE.**

<u>Conclusion of Bidding</u>

The bids have arrived, you and your Architect have thoroughly reviewed them all, you ironed out any remaining omissions throughout the Bidding Phase and now you've found them. The last addition to the project team; the one who is going to put hammer to nail and make your dream home a reality. All that remains is the "final" phase, (I argue there is an additional one) Construction Administration. (Cue melancholic music) I have none too subtly been hinting that the final phase is not the last stretch, it's a huge undertaking. It may only be one of seven phases, but it will be the most stressful, and hardest one to get through.

No Owner is happy during Construction, but almost every Owner is ecstatic when their home is built. This may seem like an extreme juxtaposition of moods, but Construction is not easy; it's messy, complicated, and intense. But if you recall one of the first things I told you when we started this journey together was thus…

**Good luck. If you keep an open mind, and you stick with this to the end, you will understand more than you ever have when its complete.**

# Part Six:

Construction Administration

*20% – 30% of Architectural Fee*

"Why am I paying an Architect during Construction? The Contractor is the one who's building my home." I heard you asking this as soon as you saw all the sub-headings in the Table of Contents. I'm going to reuse an example I gave earlier, if you were called into a courtroom you would bring a lawyer to defend you, think of the Construction Site of your new home as a courtroom, except every day can be a new "case" that will put you at risk for spending more and more money. Simply put, an Architect is your representative during Construction. They protect your interests and act as your eyes, ears and voice amidst all the chaos.

In fact, an Architect is controlling the quality of your new home before Construction even begins, but more on that later. I always spend a few meetings dispelling many myths about the Construction process when meeting with clients, so hopefully we can dispel a few of yours while we're here. First issue that always arises, how present are you expected to be as an Owner? Clients often have one of two assumptions for this:

- Stay away for the entire duration and just pray that after a few months everything will be built right. This is incorrect.
- Act as if you are a member of the Construction team and be on site every day and all times. This is also incorrect and will lead to a few polite requests to get off the site.

What is the correct answer? An agreed upon regularly occurring meeting between all parties. The Architect, Owner and Contractor should schedule a weekly meeting with a site walkthrough afterword. The Architect and Contractor will have to meet and view the site often as items arise, however the Owner should not ever be touring the site without all parties present. Many times, all parties are truly working together for a project's success. But there are antagonistic moments during the Project where a tour without anyone present will lead to some negative talk, and this only hurts the team morale and cooperation.

As huge of an undertaking as the Construction of a new home is, it truly is not a good use of your time and attention to be there every day. Large portions of the Construction will run smoothly and will be "unexciting." That is until it is not running smoothly, and then you will be able to hear the "gears" of your project grinding to a literal halt as the project runs into a "catastrophic moment that will jeopardize everything." (It often is nothing of the sort, but many in the Contracting profession have been groomed to be very dramatic at all times) If you made the mistake of venturing into Construction with no representation of an Architect, then get ready to be handed a LARGE Change Order every time this happens. If you did take my advice and have professional representation, then allow your Architect to handle these situations.

Despite all the heartache, arguments, stress and general uneasiness I often see clients suffer through, the questions answered for them at this stage come close to providing closure. Below are the last set of concerns for you to resolve:

- How are changes or "emergencies" controlled?
- How do you handle payments?
- How do you control what is used when building?

After this, it's finally done…**YOUR DREAM HOME IS BUILT AND FINALLY READY FOR YOU!**

<u>How are Changes or "Emergencies" Controlled?</u>

Things are going to come up during Construction, when doing something as complicated as building a literal building from scratch. There are a lot of factors for your Project Team to anticipate during Design, and quite a bit for your Contractor when getting your home built. During Construction, Contractors may still be issuing RFIs as these items arise. Your Architect will be responding similar to how they were during Bidding. During this phase they are no longer issuing Addendums though. They will now be responding with "Architect's Supplemental Information," or in the worst case, an "RFP."

"Architect's Supplemental Information" is just what it sounds like, it's a formal response to any issue or question that has been brought up. Often the issues that come up simply need an existing Construction Detail to be edited or even created if initially omitted. If you do not have Architectural Representation, then there will be nobody to respond to these items, you will need to rely on your Contractor to solve it. They will solve it the same way they solve everything else, by charging you more money. These Supplemental Information responses however will not only have the Architect solve it for them, but it will be done in a way that adheres to the initial Construction Contract. Thus, no additional fees should be incurred. The minor amount you had to pay your Architect to stay with you at this point could be easily been recouped with only ONE of these responses.

If changes are inevitable and something does need to be added to the scope of your Construction project, then your Architect will issue a "Request for Proposal," which is also what it sounds like. It's a formal request for the Contractor to provide a separate bid or proposal in terms of added time or money to complete the task you are asking of them. Many would argue this extra step is a waste of time rather than just having them do the work. However, anyone who has put that idea in your head is most likely profiting by that attitude. With this method, the fee will be much fairer on you, and if isn't, then their bid can be rejected. There is no shortage of other Contractors who will finish that new portion at a better price. Doctors may be allowed to bill you whatever they want after they finish, but nobody should be allowed this leverage during Construction.

At the conclusion of this part, you will have what is known as an "RFI Log," which is a database of all RFIs, Supplemental Instructions, Change Orders, RFPs and any other transfer of information during Construction. It's common for everyone to get into the swing of the project and neglect this, then months later being forced to recall a conversation had without any documentation. This never ends well, stay on top of your communication and make sure it is documented.

Communication is KEY during this phase. Keep records of everything said and get everything in writing. Often verbal agreements are thrown around all over during the many months of Construction, but nobody ever seems to remember saying things that implicate themselves or make them at fault when it comes up later. In keeping this communication open, it can greatly improve everyone's ability to manage the occasional "disasters" and disagreements. Construction is stressful, at some point you and your Contractor are going to have a heated discussion. Stay calm and consult with your Architect and the project will get built. I've seen some overwhelming obstacles that needed to be solved in projects, and they are eventually finished when calmer heads prevail. Anger and pettiness never succeeded, despite many trying.

Construction is without the doubt the most expensive purchases you are going to make. You may not have given any thought until this point, but how do you pay everyone? If you became very uncomfortable with the thought of paying for it all upfront, then good, NEVER do that. Many Contractors do care about the quality of their work and their reputation, but for just as many the only leverage you have as a client is the money they have yet to be paid.

Every Contractor is different when it comes to an initial deposit, if there is limits to what you are comfortable with then that needs to be discussed early on. How the payment for the project itself works is straightforward, as the Contractor purchases materials, pays Sub-Contractors and pays their own crew, they send an invoice to you for the amount they spent total. Whether this is bi-weekly or monthly will need to be agreed upon when signing the Contract. HOWEVER, it is in your best interest to have these invoices reviewed before money is distributed. This is typically a task for the Architect, as they are touring the site and involved with MOST Construction matters. If this sounds a bit paranoid and something that may irritate the Contractor, it's neither of those things. You hired an Architect as your representative and your money is your biggest concern needing representation. Very often, I have reviewed invoices for many materials that have been "ordered" for a project but are nowhere to be found on site. This is not an overt tactic to swindle anyone, often it is a device used to have YOU pay for the materials ahead of time. This may seem harmless enough, but you risk overpaying.

There is also the matter of withholding "Retainage" when invoices are paid. Retainage is the mandatory holding of an agreed upon percentage of each invoice to be held by you, the Owner. This is often advised to be between 5% - 10%. What is the purpose of this? As the project is ending the Contractor is going to start preparing to move on to their next job, it's how they survive. In getting ready for this new job however, they may start pulling their workers already, they may even start rushing or getting "antsy" to get off your Construction Site. This is where a lot of mistakes start happening and some lazy decisions get hastily made. Assuming you held 10% Retainage for a $300,000 project, then you have roughly $30,000 owed to the Contractor. This is the only leverage you have that can force them to stay put and finish everything correctly. You will even have a "Punch List" review, which is when your Architect tours the site with the Contractor and points out EVERY single mistake and poorly done item that needs to be redone. No matter how smooth a project has gone, this tends to be a somewhat tense site visit. The Retainage money is not released until all the items are corrected and approved by the Architect. Never be pressured to release this money too early, once it's gone so is your Contractor.

An Architect will also protect you from future legal claims when it comes to paying your invoices and final payment. An entire book could be written on handling legal matters in Construction; we will move forward assuming you followed this process and hired the right Project Team. I will point out that Construction legal matters are often resolved in a separate legal system, due to their complexity and the general lack of knowledge of the Construction process by most lawyers, judges and the general public.

To protect yourself legally, your contract must stipulate each invoice to be submitted with proof that all Sub-Contractors are being paid and up to date with their own invoices. You also need to have an "Affidavit of Lien Waivers" provided at the completion of the project. When you hire a General Contractor, you only hold a contract with them, you also only pay THEM and entrust them to pay all their employees and Sub-Contractors. I'm telling you to get proof at every invoice they are paying everyone because they are not always. If you had a fleeting thought of "that's unfortunate, but that's up to them to dispute it," then first you'll need to remove that mentality as it's a bit uncaring.

Second, it will absolutely become your problem when that unpaid Sub-Contractor files a "Lien" against your home or property. A Lien is a legal hold on your property or house that removes YOUR ownership and transfers it to the unpaid party, allowing them to collect their money. Even if you have paid the General Contractor the whole time, if they don't pay their Sub-Contractors, then they are certainly able to file a lien and sell the home or property to get paid. If that made your stomach curl in disgust then I agree with you, this is one of the worst scenarios anyone can find themselves in. So, make sure you never find yourself in this situation. I'll also briefly mention that your Architect and their Sub-Consultants have this same mechanism for getting paid, even before a project enters Construction. You may only have a set of drawings and an empty plot of land, but there is legal precedent that the design itself has improved that parcel, and if you walked away without paying your Architect then a lien can still be filed. Nobody wants to be in this situation, just make sure you pay everyone. Make your Contractor prove they are paying everyone, or else YOU are going to suffer. The "Affidavit of Lien Waivers" at project completion is a collection of sworn statements from all Sub-Contractors that they have been paid and are waiving all rights to file any liens in the future. I never like speaking emphatically, but these are the MOST important documents you could ever need. Do not give anyone any slack with these and do not pay a dime until you have these.

At the conclusion of this part, you will have a few documents for protection. You will have your Punch List report, to ensure ALL aspects of your home are finished. You will have your collection of invoices and paid receipts, to confirm everyone has been paid. You will do WHATEVER IS NECESSARY to obtain your Affidavit of Lien Waivers to ensure nobody tries to steal what you already paid for.

# How Do You Control What is Used When Building?

The Project Specifications do much more that provide an extra level of detail to your Construction Documents. They also provide clear instructions on what products, fixtures, colors, etc. you want in your home. They take this concept a step further and will clarify the steps necessary for your Contractor to submit any items they plan to use in your building to the Architect for approval. This can range from reviewing the toilet to be installed, down to what color the wood stain on the flooring will be.

This often sounds like I am describing "busy work," and while it sometimes feels this way, it's a necessary step to ensure your project meets the quality of work you paid for, this is the value of having "Submittals" reviewed by the Architect. A Contractor cannot install anything prior to receiving Approval from the Architect. The Specifications also provide what metrics any given product must meet for approval. For example, a floor tile Specification may state the color, finish, texture and size that any submitted tile must meet. As the client, you have full control over what you want in your future home and therefore what must be specified and installed.

If a Contractor does want to substitute anything, they need to not only provide the details of the proposed product, but also the cost difference. If nobody is reviewing what products are being used in your project, then it isn't hard to see that the potential for you getting ripped off has just increased. I've done many Home Inspections in which we uncover things that NOBODY would ever agree to. But if nobody is required to confirm that the contractor is using the proper material, then what is stopping them from using an inferior material for much cheaper and pocketing the cash? Ethics? Perhaps, but I and any other Architect have far too many horror stories that show otherwise. This is YOUR dream home, and an oversight on the Contractor's end should not force you to settle. No matter what complaints are raised about your selections, (and I've heard them all.) the truth is the Contractor submitted a bid committing to using what YOU wanted.

At the conclusion of this part, you will have a COMPLETED Submittal Log of all items submitted by the Contractor, and all the responses and edits issued by the Architect. Any substitution requests and their responses also need to be documented. I very rarely see a project in which all submittal items have been fully submitted. There is often the mentality that at the end of the project, this process is not as necessary. I could not disagree more, and I have plenty of examples on where this backfired for the client. Have it all reviewed, it doesn't matter if only one item is ignored, that could be the one item that causes thousands of dollars in the future.

# Conclusion of Construction Administration

It's finally built! After all the dust has cleared, (literally) you and your family can finally move in. Even though many clients have been seeing their project throughout Design and even Construction, there is always a moment of awe when they walk in for the first time with their own keys…and without dozens of Contractors hammering and sawing away in the background.

This is where many Project Teams shake each other's hands and move on to the next adventure. If I have done any justice in explaining what is involved with Construction, you can't believe that some clients try to enter Construction on their own and with no Architectural representation…I know I never can. You no doubt noticed the additional phase after this one. I included another phase for a reason, this is not the end of your Project or communication with your team.

# Part Seven:

Post Occupancy

<u>**Projects Don't End at the Handoff of Keys**</u>

I often get a confused answer when I reached out to clients a year after their project's completion. They often humored me with the small talk, thanked me for being considerate, but then really needed to know why we were speaking again. Any professional you hire should be following up with you after some time of you occupying your home. Typically, this is a year, but it may vary. What is the purpose of this follow up? To press you for more work you may want done? The thought may have crossed your mind, but that SHOULDN'T be why you're communicating again. This field is ever evolving and truly demands continual learning and adapting. Who better to provide the data of what was successful and what could have been done more effectively than you, the homeowner who spends EVERY day in the building we crafted together?

There's also the issue of your "warranty." You wouldn't buy an electronic device for twenty bucks if had a sticker saying, "All sales final," so why would your $200,000+ home not offer the same peace of mind? Let's just clarify something, you cannot return your home if you are unsatisfied, you can only sell it. But there is a one-year grace period in which things that break or are damaged are under contract to be repaired for no additional cost. I have been called to a few homes in pristine condition and less than a few months old, but with a leaking roof or a poorly installed shower fixture, etc. The first question I ask is "did you call the Contractor back?" Often, they didn't even consider it, even though the Contractor didn't build something correctly.

This of course is also assuming you made the grave mistake of not having an Architect perform a Punch List review. Many don't consider this because it's not common knowledge, and sadly most of your Contractors are always forgetful in bringing this up…Unless of course your contract does not have this warranty period built in, in which I will shake my head and wish you the best of luck. If I sound bitter, I don't mean to be, only jealous. Nobody ever hesitates to yell at their Architect, and we don't make a fraction of the profit that the Contractors do.

You can finally breath easy, you survived the Construction of a new home…Not many can make that claim, and those that have were probably not as prepared as you were.

# Epilogue:

You've Survived to Tell the Tale, Your Dream is Now a Reality

<u>Never Compromise, Never Settle, Never Give Up</u>

It's very rare when you can have a literal dream of yours be constructed into a reality, and yet here it is. The culmination of many months, constant meetings with a lot of people, and a hefty amount of money have finally produced the home of your dreams. I can recount every negative conversation or stressed out exchange with a client over the years, but for every one of them I can vividly remember the joy of bringing them into their completed building. I couldn't find a less cliché to say that, but its truth is valid. Having a project move from Design to Construction to Completion is no easy task. The difficulty of this task is not helped by the fact that many enter this realm with no guidance

However, if you stuck with me through this whole book, then you've gained a glimpse into what to expect. Did you have every one of your answers resolved in this book? I imagine you haven't, I like to think I offered some guidance to increase your confidence. But I also assume you've raised at least fifty more questions while reading.

An inquisitive attitude is what will make your project successful. I've seen so many clients become curious about Construction but get so caught up in questions and the unknown they talk themselves out of it.

It's not fair to yourself to put this much pressure on you. Unless you plan on earning your Architectural License, it's not necessary either. Consult with a professional, they will be your guide through this experience. If you consult with the right professional, they can be your teacher as well. It saddens me to no end when many people have the image of an Architect being an arrogant and impossible person to deal with, and it pains me how much we can offer these clients who never seek us out.

I didn't just write this book to hear myself talk at my computer screen for months, I did it because I want your project to transform from a collage of images you've gathered and become a true home for you and your family. I also do not want you to become a paranoid client who has been led astray from the wrong Builder, I meet with them all too often and it always disheartens me.

I want you and your home to be successful and I want it to be everything you've been dreaming of. If you read this book, (and weren't someone I forced to proofread it) then you've most likely begun wondering about that new home. Don't let that excitement or curiosity fade here though. If you need to discuss the questions you've raised, if you were wondering about some next steps or even looking to bounce some ideas of your project off someone, reach out to an Architect to get that conversation started. We do care about the quality of all the built environment improving, and your house (as well as the Residential realm in general) is no exception. If you don't think any Architects will listen, I can think of one who can't wait to hear what you're thinking of.

## <u>About the Author</u>

Bryan Toepfer is the Principal Architect and founder of TOEPFER Architecture, an Architecture firm specializing in Residential Design. When not at the office, he is collecting more accreditations and initials. He is a Licensed Architect, NCARB Certificate Holder, Certified Associate in Project Management and a Certified Asbestos Designer.

He received his Bachelor of Architectural Technology from Alfred State, and his Master of Architecture from University of Massachusetts. He went on to work in multiple firms in Vermont, Albany and Rochester in the Municipal and Commercial sectors.

He serves on the board of AIA Rochester as the Director of Government Affairs and PMI Rochester as the Director of Academic Outreach. Taking his philosophy of the importance of education to heart, he coaches Intern Architects who are taking their Licensure Exams, as well as teaching at a local university.

He resides in Rochester, New York with his wife, two cats and two dogs. When not reading the latest Batman comic or playing video games, he and his wife can be found walking the dogs or at a hockey game.